CENTRAL INK

A PRESENTATION OF DREAMS, PICTURES, STORIES, POEMS AND INSTRUCTIONS RELATING TO A JOURNEY INTO SOUL MAKING

CENTRAL INK

A Soul's Quest through Dream Work & Art©

by Marcia Lewton

Printed in Victoria, Canada

Cover art: Karen Page
Book Design and composition by Valerie Brewster, Scribe Typography
Author photo: Kathy Walker

National Library of Canada Cataloguing in Publication

Lewton, Marcia
Central ink : a soul's quest through dream work and art / Marcia Lewton.
Includes index.
ISBN 1-4120-0986-3
I. Title.
BF1078.L478 2004 154.6'3 C2003-904295-2

TRAFFORD

This book was published *on-demand* in cooperation with Trafford Publishing. On-demand publishing is a unique process and service of making a book available for retail sale to the public taking advantage of on-demand manufacturing and Internet marketing. **On-demand publishing** includes promotions, retail sales, manufacturing, order fulfilment, accounting and collecting royalties on behalf of the author.

Suite 6E, 2333 Government St., Victoria, B.C. V8T 4P4, CANADA
Phone 250-383-6864 Toll-free 1-888-232-4444 (Canada & US)
Fax 250-383-6804 E-mail sales@trafford.com
Web site www.trafford.com TRAFFORD PUBLISHING IS A DIVISION OF TRAFFORD HOLDINGS LTD.
Trafford Catalogue #03-1355 www.trafford.com/robots/03-1355.html

10 9 8 7 6 5 4 3 2

For my families of origin:
Duncans, Faulkners, Pottages, and Morrises.

Contents

Part 4: In the Depths

Part 5: Coming Back Up

DREAMS

POEMS

STORIES

ART

Preface

In the Gnostic Gospel of Thomas, Jesus is said to have urged people to bring forth what is within, so that it will save them. If you do not do so, he warned, what is within will destroy you. These words speak about a necessary spiritual task, redemptive when engaged, destructive if ignored.

But what does it mean to bring forth what is within?

No doubt this passage can be interpreted in more than one way: to unburden oneself of a secret, to perceive and speak a truth, to free a suppressed emotion, to develop one's gifts, and more.

Here the text will be taken to mean all of these, and especially, in addition, to make conscious what has been hidden, to access unconscious material by various means, especially dreams. This work, as a daily spiritual practice, leads to what the poet, John Keats, considered soul-making.

There are a number of ways to work with dreams. I will demonstrate or explain the ones I use, but a reader must keep in mind that there are many. A short bibliography of resources on dream work can be found at the end of this book.

For me, in addition to the dream work itself, there was a further task that is in keeping with my own sense of purpose, the task of creating a coherent presentation of the material in order to demonstrate a way of working and to give an example of what can happen when one undertakes a process of this depth.

I have written and published a number of stories and poems since I began writing when I was in my mid-thirties but have always had to struggle with creative blocks of varying degrees of obduracy. In recent years I stopped publishing fiction and poetry and engaged all my efforts in soul work in hopes of encouraging the free flow of creative energy. *Central Ink* is the story of that project-in-progress.

The title, *Central Ink*, came from the first dream I had when I began engaging in dream work. It laid bare what is perhaps the deepest issue of my life. Here it is:

THE CENTRAL INK DREAM

> I approach and enter an octagonal building made of cedar shakes with a conical roof. Although it is only a small hut on the outside, it is much larger inside, like a spacious pavilion. It now has central ink. Central ink, like central heating.
>
> The ink comes from a deep well in the center like a fountain. It flows into spokes of varying lengths, which radiate outward from the center. There are places to sit all around, stone work benches, and the central ink is available to each bench. It seems as much like fuel as liquid. It burns with a black flame, and sometimes it's malleable, but shiny, like anthracite, for the sculptors. There are mailboxes at the ends of the central ink spokes.
>
> The lights are low; it's shadowy here. The atmosphere is quiet and peaceful. No one else is present.

The task implicit in this scene is for me to sit down at one of those benches, one near the center, to use the black ink/fuel welling up from below, and to use one of the mailboxes to make my work available to those others who would be interested.

When I was a little girl in school, my teacher put the following verse on the blackboard, and I learned it as I did all the other verses and ditties of childhood to remember at odd moments in later years. At the time, I thought it was just another self-improvement verse about diligence. As

I grew older, however, I realized that soul-satisfying work was not an onerous chore imposed by the boss or by the desire for money or fame. I noticed what a treasure such work could be, and I understood that Henry Van Dyke wrote not an exhortation but a prayer.

> Let me but do my work from day to day,
> In field or forest; at the desk or loom,
> In roaring marketplace or tranquil room.
> Let me but find it in my heart to say,
> When vagrant wishes beckon me astray,
> "This is my work, my blessing, not my doom.
> Of all who live, I am the one by whom
> This work can best be done in the right way."
>
> From *Work*, by Henry Van Dyke

This book is an attempt to answer the prayer and fulfill the dream.

The project began taking shape in my imagination when I was suffering from the effects of three significant losses, beginning with the greatest loss of my life, the illness and death of my husband. His death was followed a few months later by the loss of my work in the community, due to the cancellation of the local incest survivors' support program that had provided me with challenging and rewarding work as a group facilitator. And finally I found myself struggling to recover my physical mobility in the aftermath of surgery for a knee injury. Deeply depressed, I was not fit to take part in community life, so I looked inward for rehabilitation. What resources did I have? What skills?

The obvious answer was that my greatest resource was the imaginative work I had already done, and that my greatest skill was the literary ability to write it down. I felt ready, even eager, to use the wealth of material I had been gathering these past several years, but I was afraid I would encounter the same resistance against presentation that I already knew so well. In the throes of a creative block, what has been considered a wealth of material becomes a heap of worthless trash fit only for the burn pile or the shredder. But since I couldn't know ahead what I would encounter, there was nothing to do but begin.

I did this by gathering preliminary dreams and other works of imagination in the hope that they would shed light on my *readiness* to do it, my readiness for what I felt deeply called to do yet found difficult to begin. Would my inspiration be hampered once again by the spirit killers who all too often undermined my efforts from within? Were there any countervailing forces that could encourage me to carry this project through to a happy ending? Would there ever be a happy ending that did not precede another difficult beginning?

Several times, before going to sleep, I asked for images that would further the process. I promised that I would treat any images presented as meaningful. I would tease out their relevance to my request. I would also relate them to earlier dreams and artworks in order to create not just a thread of meaning but a pattern.

I have deliberately omitted dates from the dreams and artworks presented. Inner work does not follow a chronological or linear pattern. Many folks liken its progress to a spiral. I myself think it's more like the pattern you see if you watch clothes tumbling in a washing machine: up comes the red sock; here's the flowered pillowcase again; the raveling on one shirt catches the button on the next, etc.

Inner work does not come to an end. No matter how long you "bring forth what is within," there is always more to bring forth, and it is almost always connected to something you've already brought forth time and time again.

"You'll never finish your book," whispers the flowered pillowcase. "It will go on and on forever." I've heard that kind of talk before. I let the red sock answer: "So what?"

The first dream came immediately, but it was so obscure and nonsensical that I almost gave up without beginning. I realized that even with an interpretation for the dream, anyone reading it would need to know something of my personal history to make sense of it, but I didn't want to write an autobiography: born, grew up, did this, did that, blah blah blah. I wanted to write a book about the life of imagination.

But a promise is a promise, and breaking a promise to the source of dreams is a serious matter. Once unconscious forces are invoked, the price for not respecting them can be high. And so I began.

CENTRAL INK

PART I

Getting Ready

CHAPTER 1

Playing Card Messages

PLAYING CARD MESSAGES

> In the dream, I am the involuntary sender of a message to an unknown recipient. The message is a playing card, hearts somewhere between six and ten.
>
> Now I'm *receiving* playing card messages, one after the other, each a bit more alarming than the last. Finally one comes telling me that my husband Vance and his new wife will soon come to get the car.

Wondering what insights this odd little dream would yield, I began by examining each image and writing down the associations that occurred to me. This is only one way of many to work with a dream, but it is easy and it often brings results.

Associations

I: The very first image in the dream is the "I". One does not easily realize that the "I" in a dream is only a part of the whole person dreaming the dream. Sometimes the "I" is called the "ego image" or the "dream ego", either of which is more accurate. It makes for clumsy reading, however. With these factors in mind, I am choosing to call the ego image of the dream "I", while asking the reader to keep in mind what is meant.

INVOLUNTARY SENDER OF A MESSAGE: The specific "I" here is identified as someone who is involuntarily sending a message to an unknown recipient. This calls to mind my identity as a writer. Anyone who writes and publishes sends messages to strangers, messages that often contain material that the writer doesn't intend to put out there. By making my personal material public, I could be sending a message I don't understand to a person I don't know.

RECEIVING MESSAGES: The possible response to being public is alarming, for fear of drawing hostile replies.

But taking the dream literally is only one possibility. After all, I had specifically asked for this dream, and therefore had sent a message to the powers within of my intent to make this most personal work public.

Considered as a picture of my inner situation at the time, the dream is actually pretty clear. There are two scenes in this little drama: in the first I am sending a message contained in a playing card specified as "hearts, between six and ten." In the second I find out that I am going to be not only without my husband but without my vehicle as well.

Often (but not always) the second scene in a dream is a result of what happens in the first scene, just as it is in a play.

Thus a good hypothesis might be that the loss of husband and car follows inevitably the information contained in the message "hearts, between six and ten."

VANCE AND HIS NEW WIFE: Another cautionary note is in order here. Just as the dream ego as "I" is only part of the dreamer, so are all the other non-ego characters in the dream. The non-ego characters are less conscious parts of the dreamer, and they are dressed up as familiar or stereotypical characters to help the dreamer identify them.

As I write this, my actual husband, Vance, has been dead for several years. He was not only my husband but also much more, including supporter of my creative work, especially writing. It is in his supportive position behind this work that he usually appears as a dream figure; indeed, it was this work that drew us together at the beginning. If he has a new wife in my dream, then the "I" who does creative work and sends messages does not have his support.

His withdrawal indicates that—because of "hearts, between six and ten"—I lack the full backing of a quality I need in order to "do my work from day to day." I think of this quality as "drive." It's the ability to maintain steam, to go the distance. In dreams it has been represented by fuel, juice, alcoholic spirits, money, and by the helpful male figure solidly behind me.

As a fiction writer, I've received my share of rejection slips. One of them contained a comment that hurt my feelings—at first. On the polite printed slip, the editor had scrawled, "Lacks cohesive thrust." But after a time, I came not only to share the phrase with Vance in jokes but also to see it as a precise definition of my condition. I do indeed lack cohesive thrust. When Vance was alive and strong, I borrowed it from him. Without him, I need to find it within myself, again and again.

As I write this, the conditions of my life are very rewarding. I have everything I need for a happy life. But I am pressed from within to take on the task of putting this material together for presentation, even though the task is difficult, and even though I shake my head in wonderment at why anyone would take it on. Why not simply dismiss this call to work and do something else instead?

TAKING MY CAR: No more drive. No more ability to move.

Cars are common images in dreams. They mean different things to different people, just as waking life cars do. People move around the world in different ways, and the cars in the dreams often reflect one's style at the time of the dream.

The image of my car's being taken away indicates that change is coming. The popular view is that change is for the better, that it can be willed, that it's enjoyable. I have not found this to be true. Change requires sacrifice, and very few of us make significant sacrifices easily. To change enough for it to be portrayed as yielding one's car feels just like it sounds. The driveway is empty. This is not something to take lightly.

The self-help books tout change as betterment. In 1910, a French pharmacist, Emile Coué, suggested repeating the affirmation, "*Every day, in every way, I'm growing better and better.*" This grew into a belief that saying it made it true, and people began muttering it wherever they went. Such affirmations can help people balance the negative thoughts that plague them, but the human condition of ups and downs makes it clear that it doesn't bear scrutiny as an overall truth. So it pays, when change is in the offing, to prepare for a trip into the unknown, for better or worse.

My car, my usual vehicle, might also refer to this book, or to writing in general as the vehicle I use for self-expression. Will unconscious forces portrayed as Vance with a new wife take it away from me? As a later section will reveal, the car is an important symbol for me.

Or maybe I won't let them take the car. I could throw a tantrum and refuse. I could dispose of the new wife, tell Vance he has no business with another woman, as I certainly would if he were alive and I were awake. I could abandon the whole project in a fit of pique.

The dream doesn't give me this option. My sense is that Vance would hold firm here. Indeed, as I ask him in my imagination what's going on, he replies immediately. "Hell," he says, "you're not using the damn car. I might as well take it. You're sitting there with involuntary messages flying back and forth. Talk about lacking cohesive thrust! Maybe if you wake up and get some focus going, I'll dump the new wife and bring the car home."

The inner Vance gets disgusted with me and stomps off from time to time. When one part of me gets disgusted and stomps off, my mobility slows way down. But I am not conscious enough about what's happening to be able to do anything about it. Vance's strong language is an attempt to wake me up.

PLAYING CARDS: Here, I believe, is the key to the dream's meaning. A short time before this dream occurred, I had written not an autobiography but an imaginative rendering of the relevant facts of my history in a little story, called *Daughter of Hearts, Daughter of Clubs*. It was written using the playing card motif. I believe that the dream was referring to this story. Six through ten were the years of my life when things happened to my heart and left me with a particular set of difficulties.

Just as dreams lead to artworks so do artworks lead to dreams, as may be the case here. One need not be skilled to produce the artworks that so enrich one's inner life. They need never be shown to anyone, need never become objects of pride or shame; they need only to be *done* to have their effect. A sheet of paper and a box of crayons are all it takes, and the willingness to let the hand make manifest what has arisen in the imagination.

When you take an interest in what springs spontaneously into imagination by making something material to represent it: a drawing, a poem, a ritual, a different way of acting, then the imagination will reward you by taking an interest in you.

What follows is a description of my life in the Playing Card Family.

Daughter of Hearts, Daughter of Clubs

Once upon a time in a land where people worked hard and were poor anyway a baby girl was sent to the Peg of Hearts and the Tight Fist of Clubs, who needed something to focus on besides their work, their poverty, and the storms of their marriage.

They had been married for several years now, and since the Peg was at heart a Heart and the Fist a Club through and through, the very qualities that had first attracted them to each other had now turned into faults that were making them miserable. Her vivacity aroused his fear that she would seduce other men, and his frugality, along with the stay-at-home lifestyle he favored, was making her feel trapped instead of secure.

The in-laws added fuel to the blaze. The Hearts included the Peg in their feasts and festivities, and the Clubs, who lived right next door to the couple, kept track of her comings and goings and reported back to the Fist. Even her job put her under suspicion: the laughing and joking, the friendships, the possibility of flirtations or worse.

The little girl didn't want to belong to this couple. She was hoping for an easy-going family with lots of kids and parents who got along.

But she wasn't given a choice. The only choice she had was at the moment of her birth, whether to hang back for a few more minutes or to follow the urging of her Destiny.

"Snap it up!" said Destiny, nudging her toward the door of the bloody dark. "It's almost midnight."

"So what?" she spit back. "This is not a story about a pumpkin."

"That's what you think. If you don't make it out of here before the clock strikes twelve, you'll be cast as a Friday's Child, one more Loving and Giving female, boring boring boring, for this whole circle of the mortal coil. That sure sounds to me like nothing to eat but pumpkin, boiled and broiled and baked and fried."

"Oh," she said. "And if I hurry?"

"A Thursday's Child has Far to Go. Need I say more?"

So out she slid, with two minutes to spare. They named her Carrie. She would carry their hopes, their care, their disappointments, their fears and ambitions, their battleground.

As a Thursday's Child, Carrie brought with her a particular birthright of talents and energy. Destiny had tucked it into her hand as she emerged: the wherewithal she would need for her journey, a goodly sum, for she had Far to Go.

When the new parents saw what their child brought with her, they congratulated themselves for having produced this well-endowed little being, and once or twice they even congratulated each other. But mostly they acted true to form, struggling for control of Carrie and her birthright of energy and talents.

Her father immediately invested a large amount of the energy in a rigid Maintenance Schedule that would strictly regulate all matters pertaining to Carrie's health and upbringing. The Schedule was an expensive item, and he wanted to clamp down on the rest of the birthright to keep it out of harm's way, but her mama seized a comparable amount from the talent hoard for Performance studies that would develop her little daughter into a child she could be proud of. Between the two of them, her parents dipped deeply into Carrie's traveling fund—for her own good, of course.

Also living in the home during part of Carrie's early years was a boy in his early teens, the Drum of Spades, a son of her mama's from her previous marriage to a Spade. Sometimes he was there and sometimes not, for Carrie's father did not like having a stepson around and did not make the teen-ager welcome, but when he was there, he too encouraged Carrie's Performance studies. He took out bragging rights and showed her off, saying, "My sister this" and "My sister that" and shining in her smart-little-girl glory.

And there was glory, albeit in a small circle. Carrie's birthright included a number of talents that could be polished to dazzle an audience and to keep up her mama's reputation as the best of the Heart sisters, the others having snot-nosed children, not too bright, and to show up the Clubs, whose children were smart enough and clean, but dull. Carrie managed to be both lively and smart and to know how to use a handkerchief when the Heart family nose acted up.

The bulk of her talents and energy went in this way, to further her father's Maintenance Schedule and her mama's yearning for something to be proud of. Carrie did not realize what was happening. Her only clue was an occasional yank on her ears by Destiny, who would warn her to keep something back for her journey, not to let them have it all. But children born with the resources to follow their path are not necessarily born knowing they have those resources. She had forgotten Destiny, and the yanks on her ears produced nasty infections that brought down the wrath of the Fist upon the Peg for getting lax about the Schedule that was supposed to keep Carrie in perfect health.

The little girl soon learned what she had to do to keep the Fist from hammering on the Peg: she had to keep things from happening to her. Her father's threat to her mama, "If anything happens to Carrie, you're out," made her desperate to avoid trouble of any kind. Having her beloved Peg kicked out of the house would leave her alone with her father and whatever dull Club relatives he installed to see to her care. What a dismal prospect! The Clubs had no sense of fun, no sense of beauty, no drama, no color, no song. Their entire attention was on frugality, maintenance, and schedule, and that was no life for Carrie. She made a solemn, unbreakable vow to herself: "I'll do anything, anything, whatever it takes, to keep my mama from being kicked out."

She soon saw the need for another task on her mama's behalf. The Peg had missed the bus as far as accomplishments and achievements were concerned. Poor and working by the age of fourteen, married with a child by eighteen, divorced a short time later and working harder than ever to support the child, she had married into the Club family hoping to improve her situation. But look what she was stuck with instead! She still had to work unrewarding jobs because she'd missed the bus on education, still had to support the son because she had missed the bus on contraception, and was now married to this intolerable Fist with his never-ending frugality and devotion to schedule. Carrie believed that she had been sent to make up to her mama for her disappointments.

And so her birthright went. Carrie practiced her Performances with diligence and presented them to her mother, who praised her and smiled on her with great devotion.

When her big half-brother was around, he too rewarded her performances with his attention. She became "his girl" and she loved him much better than she did her grouchy Tight Fist of a father. The Fist, taking note of her devotion to the Drum, kept a jealous eye out for any funny stuff, always checking up, always clamping down.

One day when Carrie was with her big brother in his room, there was a loud banging on the door. "What's going on in there?" yelled the angry Fist, bursting into the room. The rest was chaos. Carrie remembered it as everything flying apart and the house falling down. The next time she saw inside the door of the Drum's room, all his things were gone, his bed stripped down to the bare gray mattress.

She went to her own room. It was dreary and still. Her brother was gone forever. Her mama's days were probably numbered too. Carrie wished she were dead.

But of course a little girl doesn't wish something like that for very long. To cheer herself up, she went to her closet and took out her favorite dress, red and silky and a little bit shiny, a gift from her Grandma Heart. She put it on and added her black patent leather tap dancing shoes.

She was in front of the mirror twirling the full skirt of her red silk dress when her father again appeared at the door. Like a storm he descended upon her and tore the red dress from collar to hem, yanking it off as he tumbled her around, yelling about "trash like your mother." When she came to rest in a corner of the room, she watched, horrified, as he ripped her dress into chunks and strips, the sash here, the lace there, frayed silk threads falling on the braided rug, everything falling apart.

It was not long afterwards that Carrie's wish to die was almost granted. Coming home from school one day, she felt weaker and weaker, and sicker and sicker, until at last she could not walk any farther. From there she crawled the rest of the way home.

She was sick for a long, long time. She had to stay in bed, reading and making designs with a compass, holding it all together. (See picture, page 17.) But she didn't die. Instead, she responded to the chiding of her forgotten friend, Destiny, who told her firmly, "You can't check out yet, kid. You're not even on the road. You've got traveling to do." Reluctantly she regained her strength and rejoined the life of the household.

But she made herself a second promise, another solemn vow, after surviving the whole ordeal. "This is never going to happen to me again," she swore. "Never ever again." No more "his girl." No more red dress. She would wrap razor wire around herself from now on to hold everything together. No matter that it cost her another huge chunk of her birthright of energy to keep it in place.

And so she ventured out to seek her fortune. The razor wire was not visible. She looked good in blue and thus did not miss wearing the red dress.

Years passed. A suitor, the Hard Work of Diamonds, courted Carrie. They soon married and settled into life together, where they lived in a fine big house that brought pleasure to her mama as well as to Carrie herself. She bore two little daughters who were endowed with the finest Heart qualities: gaiety, humor, energy, brilliance, and great sensitivity of feeling.

And then when the little girls were half grown, the Peg died. Carrie went into grief and shock. What could her life be now, without her mama to offer delicacies to?

The funeral was no more than over when Destiny started agitating again. "What have you got to lose?" he asked. "Your mama's gone now. You don't have to protect her from the Fist any longer. You don't have to make up for her missing the bus. You can start your journey."

"Not possible," she answered. "My birthright's been ruined. I don't know how to use my energy and my talents for myself, only for them. It's all squandered."

"You'll just have to travel cheap then," he said. "Without talents. On a low energy budget. But you'd better hurry. You're starting to slide toward the nursing home."

He was right. Carrie had already begun to notice.

Very cautiously she began adding red to her wardrobe, a scarf, red shoes, trying out what she called "the New Me." Earrings. Curly hair. Full skirts.

Before long she attracted the attention of the Fist, who growled at her and said once again, "Just like your mother," in a tone that meant he didn't like it.

But by then she had also attracted someone else's attention. She was meeting him for midday walks in the botanical garden and on the wooded grounds of the art museum. Soon they fell in love, Carrie and the Voice of Hearts.

There was a long period of great uproar, years in fact, with much thrashing about, as marriages were stretched open and couples realigned: Carrie with the Voice, and the Voice's wife, the Zest of Hearts, with Carrie's husband, the Work of Diamonds. Such stress on the beams of being!

But for Carrie, there was no turning back; this love was part of her journey.

As the two lovers traveled together, more years passed. Carrie developed new talents and learned new ways to manage energy. More roads opened up. Her daughters grew into womanhood and went out in the world to seek their own fortunes.

For many years Carrie and the Voice spent happy times together, as well as sharing the disagreements and troubles that came along the way. She wore red often, and the razor wire became less binding as time went on and she tried to dismantle it to keep from hurting her beloved. The Voice of Hearts was her ally as well as her playmate.

But as happens with everyone, she would always carry the burdens of her childhood and the scars of her parents' war. And when the worst thing possible finally happened and the Voice grew sick and died, she was left alone to bear them by herself.

"Very well then," she thought, reeling from the blows that rained down on her. "If this is the way it is, this is the way it is." And she hunkered down and sat tight, and when she needed to move but it hurt too much, she did the thing she had done that day long ago when she was too sick to walk home from school. "If I can't walk, I'll crawl."

For a long time Carrie struggled along through the mud, inch by hard-fought inch. Surely things were supposed to be better than this! Surely there was a way to have a happy ending.

But no, she knew better. To find a happy ending, she would need help, and there was no help out there. Whatever she needed, she would have to find or create for herself.

And then one day she heard someone whistling off to her side. Someone was there, though she couldn't see who it was. Another day she felt bushes tremble, and when she came to a thorn branch, an unseen hand lifted it for her. Tears came to her eyes.

A familiar voice said, "You don't really have to create the ground in front of you to take the next step." It was Destiny.

"Oh yes I do!" she answered, halting with one foot stopped in mid air.

"You know this journey isn't over yet, don't you?"

She had been wondering if her Destination was nothing more than the mud she'd been struggling through for so long. She lowered her foot and took another step.

"Remember the Central Ink Hut?" he asked. "That's where you've been heading, whether you knew it or not, since you were a little girl."

The Central Ink Hut was a place she had seen deep in a dream: an eight-sided building with a conical roof, small from the outside, very large within. From a well in the center poured ink, Central Ink, like central heating, that radiated through a set of pipes like the burners of a gas range to workbenches all around the room. The well went deep, and the ink burned with a black flame.

Surely Destiny was not talking about this, was he? "The Central Ink hut?" she asked. "My Destination?"

"Yes, ma'am," he answered.

She took his hand, feeling his support as they walked. Maybe they would reach the Hut. And maybe inside would be the ink and the tools she would use to do the work that was hers to do on this earth.

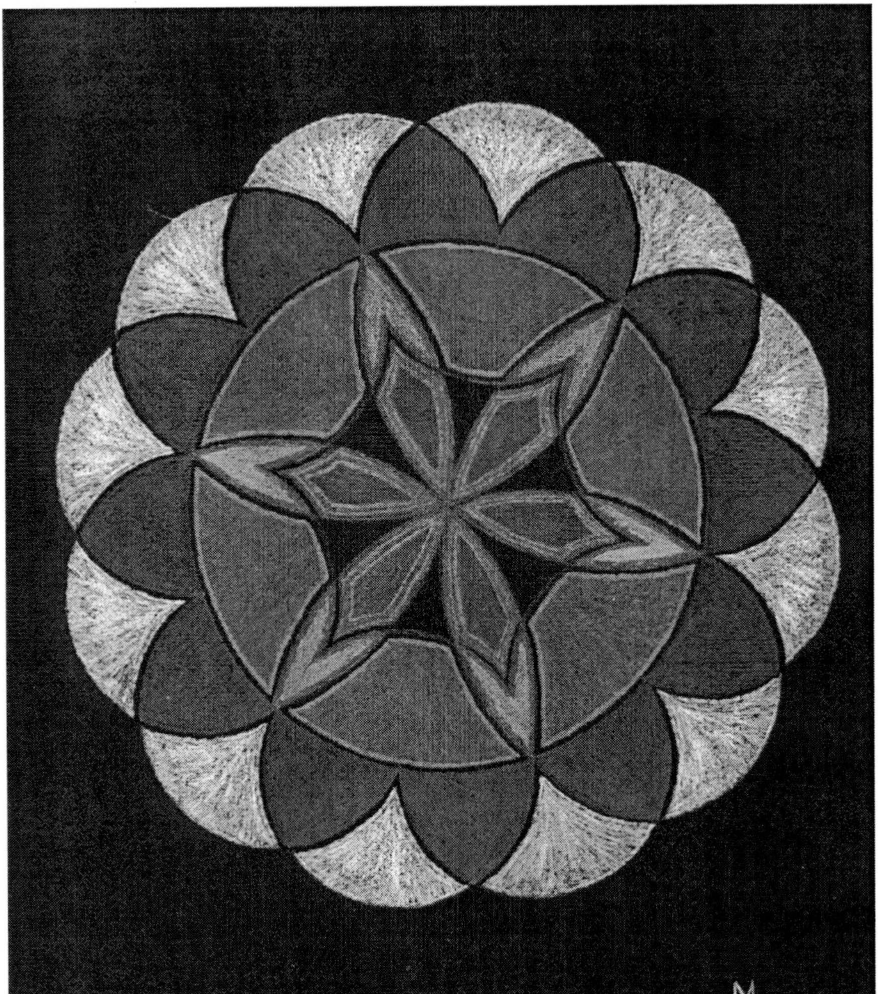

Holding It All Together

CHAPTER 2

A Different Point of View

The next asked-for dream was a lot more fun and led me into a fruitful excursion. It reminded me that dream work, though serious, need not be solemn. Dreams often make use of jokes, puns, and hilarious scenes to make their point.

WRITING GREAT UTTERANCES

> In this dream I am in third person, and funnier. I view myself with tolerance as the woman in the story. Life as it is being lived in the present moment is part of her story, not part of my struggle.
>
> This woman, *I myself in third person*, has added a spa to her house. To accommodate the spa, she has to install it in a separate structure, which I think is simply a mobile home. Then she decides that if she has a spa, she has to balance it by having a library as well, which means still another mobile crammed onto the property. She then sits in her studio and writes what she believes are great utterances, only they don't make sense. This writing is turned out automatically. Her favorite is a two-word exhortation

"Churn, Vern!," which she utters frequently. I think she is addressing the instigator of this *lingua primavera.*[1]

Comments

What fun! If this is what working in the Central Ink Hut is like, I could enjoy it thoroughly. A spa for the body, a library for the mind, a studio for the imagination. Not having to worry about making sense. All I have to do when difficulties threaten is to cry out, "Churn, Vern!" and the words pour forth.

Fiction writers know that writing a story in third person creates a distance that a first person narration cannot achieve. When the story is told by a character in first person, an "I", the story's vision is limited to what the "I" him or herself can perceive. Switching to third person, with the character being a "he" or a "she", the distance between the character and the storyteller is greater, giving the latter a much wider view of the circumstances.

This point will be made frequently here. In life as in fiction it helps to open the view to a wider angle, to watch what's going on rather than staying mired in what one feels.

The fact that the woman in the dream is "in third person" harks back to an imaginary search for koi that began with an even earlier dream. The use of the word "koi" in the dream was odd. I have never seen koi, but I imagine them as gold colored. In a dream, such fish would be precious gold soul fragments. Here's the dream:

IN THE PUBLIC MARKET, LOOKING FOR KOI

I'm in a huge public market in a strange city. The market is thronged with people shopping at the many stalls and pushing their way through the crowds.

A little barefoot girl is crying nearby. Maybe she's lost.

1. *Lingua primavera* is an invented phrase using "lingua," which means tongue or language, and "primavera," which refers to chopped vegetables, as in a primavera sauce.

I offer to help her, and she shows me her hurt foot. One of her tiny toes has a swollen lump on it with a splinter sticking out.

I'm going to need to find some tweezers to remove the splinter, so I seat her on a stool at a table in an open section of the market where people eat. Both the table and the stool are solidly attached to the floor. I put a large pot of food, something with little chunks of chicken, on the adjacent stool so she can reach it easily, and I tell her to wait here while I go find some tweezers.

As I push through the crowds I ask people if they have tweezers I could use for a moment; I stop at stalls to see if I could buy a pair. After several disappointments, I begin to wonder if I could pull the splinter out with my fingers.

A couple of times during this search I see my partner (probably Vance) and we have some conversation. It's indistinct and ill remembered, but it concerns his trying to convince me that it's okay for him to go out with other women. He tells me that it would happen only when I am otherwise occupied, such as the time he took someone to an afternoon performance at the symphony. I am disgusted with him. I'll have none of it. It's not okay. And I don't want to be bothered with this issue right now.

Now I'm at an outdoor derelict part of the market. The buildings have crumbled away and the area is overgrown with tall grasses. I stumble along. There are rings of cut stone underfoot, old pools about a yard in diameter, most of them filled in with dirt and high grass, but some still holding water. I ask a man if there are any koi in them. His answer is ambiguous: he doesn't say yes or no but he leads me on as though to show me something.

A mosquito has bitten my leg and raised a huge itchy knot. I follow the man, scratching and hoping I won't be eaten alive.

Comments

As soon as I find myself in the public market, that is, looking toward the daunting possibility of public presentation, I come upon an injured, lost little girl.[2] My first task is to take care of her, comfort her and feed her and try to attend her injury, which, fortunately, is not life threatening. In the process I argue with Vance about his involvement with another woman. Maybe this is the "new wife" referred to in PLAYING CARD MESSAGES; maybe the new wife is a part of me who needs to be taken to nourishing places like the symphony. But not in this dream, which finally ends with the image of being led into the area of round pools that may or may not have koi in them and being bitten by a mosquito.

Many experts on dreams would agree that a round pool with golden fish in it refers to our central core, our true self, the place where we reflect the image of divinity with the greatest clarity, where our destiny lies, urging us to live it. Doing inner work is a search for the gold, that most valuable thing that is the meaning of one's life. Going into the public marketplace, then, could lead me to the gold.

This gold is not money or acclaim. It is the satisfaction of fulfilling your destiny, of living the life you know deeply that you're supposed to live.

Once in a while I dream of being bitten by mosquitoes. I believe this image goes back to seeing a TV documentary in which a man so badly wanted wildlife photographs for his story that he set up a blind in the wilderness and stayed in it even while being devoured by mosquitoes. This project must have been necessary to the fulfilling of his destiny. Nothing wrong with *his* cohesive thrust!

A few days after having that dream, I happened upon a quote on death and dying from John Donne that contained the phrase: "in a sullen weedy lake" which I then used as the starting point for a piece of writing:

2. Lost, hurt little girl. Yes, it's the scorned figure of the "inner child" but don't reject her out of hand as psychobabble. She's not a generic inner child; she's particular, just as all of them are if you really listen when they contact you. They are figures, not figments, of the imagination, inner persons that symbolize or represent aspects of yourself.

WHAT THE GOLDEN FISHES SAY

In a sullen weedy lake the koi swim cautiously. Through slimy stems they nose their way. When the surface thrums with the landing of a fly, they wiggle upward.

But this splash is too resounding to be a fly. It's a woman come to join them. They nibble her toes, her fingers, her eyelids. She feels their kisses.

She is looking for a happy ending.

She is now fish food, the true savor of which was unknown to her before. But her flaws are her blessings, and her ability to feel what others feel now helps her taste her own flesh as the koi feast upon it. How did she come to be so delicious? The fish tear into her until there's nothing left but bones.

The bones now lie in a heap on the bottom of the sullen weedy lake. The koi visit them often, remembering.

"To have a happy ending," they say, "you have to shift your point of view."

Comments

To be "myself in third person" I have to follow the advice of the golden fish. But to shift my point of view to that of the fish that are eating me?

So, what's eating me? And how do things look from *that* point of view?

At least I'm getting some information about what this odyssey requires. One thing it requires is to look at myself "in third person," that is, from a different point of view, as a player in a drama in which I may or may not be the star.

Many people approach dream work as an aid to achieving ego goals, believing that the ego, or conscious identity, is what one really is. A wider perspective allows an exploration of the other aspects of the self that play such an important, if unconscious, role in one's life.

CHAPTER 3

Trash on the Floor

The next few dreams called my attention to a habit of nit-picking reluctance to let go of things at the *good enough* point. I want things put together *right*, and I want the loose ends tied up. Dream work requires attention to the details even while being open-ended in all directions. But could it be that trying to catalogue and dissect every image in every dream might hamper the current project, the book you are now reading?

PREPARING FOR A PUBLIC READING

I am getting ready for a semi-formal event, a public presentation, probably a poetry or fiction reading, in an enormous old house. Vance is helping me. I leave to go find some bottles of spirits, different kinds in interesting bottles.

When I return, Vance is waiting outside the house, which is now locked up. I try a back door and discover that it's a Dutch door and the bottom half is unlocked. Vance starts to unlock the top, but I have already crouched down and gone through.

Inside, I see that he has been busy. The room where the event is being staged is very large and wood-paneled, with a dark-colored wood floor. Vance has dragged chairs and couches in and arranged them in semi-circular rows facing the podium. He hasn't gone so far as to sweep the floor, however, and it's a bit dusty with several pieces of litter, including a clear cellophane or plastic package from a snack of some kind. I am touched and amused by what he has and hasn't done.

Associations

PUBLIC EVENT: a literary event like many I've participated in, both as facilitator and as reader. The semi-formal setting here implies an intimate audience, my favorite kind.

HELP FROM VANCE: Vance was a man who served art, who took the art process seriously, acted as a steward, a helper of artists. Here he's with the writer part of me wholeheartedly, giving his support to the public presentation.

GOING OUT FOR SPIRITS: finding where the spirit is bottled up. In a much earlier dream the same bottled up spirit was depicted as *juice*, which was bottled up in jugs embedded in a crumbling brick basement wall, implying that considerable ingenuity would be required to get it out in a usable form.

Spirits & Hearts & Dirt on the Floor was one of the possible titles I considered for this book. The theme of spirit is a constant throughout, and it is with considerable regret that I must trim out many dreams on the subject.

I think of the whole person as made up of four parts. In addition to the usual three: the thinking part or *mind*; the feeling and valuing part or *heart*; and the acting part or *body*; I add *soul*, the imagining part, the part that has been neglected in our achievement-oriented society. *Spirit* is something else entirely. It comes from without, as life, or breath, or inspiration. A spiritual practice, such as dreamwork, connects the body, mind, heart, and soul to act in conjunction with this inspiration.

DUTCH DOOR: It can be opened at the top or the bottom with the other half left closed, which suggests a partial passageway between the inner and the outer worlds. A house that was mine for many years had such a door that opened between a large screened porch and a sunroom where the Writers' Center held its Board meetings, where many literary events were planned.

BACK DOOR: entering the public-event place quietly, modestly, even surreptitiously, without fuss. Entering this way, like a child ducking through the bottom half of a Dutch door, introduces the important element of play into the mix.

This means of entrance into the public-event place appeals to my desire to be unobtrusive and playful, to duck in quickly without making a grand entrance. When I can ease into the public arena through a back door, with no fuss or fanfare, I do not arouse my powerful inhibition against self-presentation.

DEBRIS ON THE FLOOR: a common theme in my dreams; not a personal mess; not a large mess; the detritus of the past; the leftover mess that never gets completely cleaned up.

POWER IS NOT FOR SWEEPING

> In this dream I am using an electric broom, trying to sweep up some bits of litter. Nothing is happening; the cord has become detached from the appliance. I check the outlet and find that it has shorted out and is blackened and sparking. I pull the plug out and the sparking subsides.
>
> Now I'm in bed with Vance, making love with him behind me. It feels wonderful. I move and push against him to get to the place that feels best. My movements bring him to orgasm. After awhile he twists the upper part of his body around me so that we are holding each other face-to-face while still joined front to back, an impossible but wonderful position.

Comments

Because of the image of sweeping the floor and the loss of electric current, this dream is about more than a bodily desire for sex. Dreams often use sexual imagery as a metaphor for the coming together that has to occur for the life force to continue.

When nit-picking the floor stops, my libido becomes available for erotic union. My beloved is behind me, not off in my car with another wife. Fertilization can take place. The following poem of mine addresses the need to make oneself available for the fertilizing image in order to end the emptiness of a block:

WAITING FOR THE HEADLESS DRAGONS[3]

When the afternoon sky is a fruitless bowl
and the eye in your dream sees nothing at all,
dress yourself in silks
and go lie down
in a field
where there is corn.

Lie first on your face.
Hide.
Hold a cornstalk
in your strong right hand.
Hold it at the crown
tightly
where its roots are cables in clay.
You are safe now.
Be still.

3. "Waiting for the Headless Dragons" from *In The Heart of Town, Still Digging*, Barnwood Press. The title refers to Hexagrams 1 *The Creative* and 2 *The Receptive* of the *I Ching*. When one throws nines in all six lines of Hexagram 1, the whole hexagram changes in to #2, a fertilizing sequence. A commentary refers to a flight of dragons without heads.

Soon the clock in your ear will stop thumping.
Soon
behind your eyelids
where there was only the merciless sun
you will see a tree hung with apples.
You will notice the pain of a small stone
against your forehead.
When this happens,
turn over
and rest.

Now
open your eyes.
Look up through the corn.
Through clattering leaves
you will see tassels
painting clouds
in the sky.

Be still
and feel the weight of pollen raining,
raining.

CHAPTER 4

Longing for the Sacred

James Hillman, post-Jungian psychologist, provocative author, and father of Archetypal Psychology, speaks of soul as being at the very top of the list of human values, right up there with life itself and divinity.

Doing soul work is a *sacred* task, a spiritual discipline. It uses the imagination to attempt connection with what is deepest within, which leads to the connection with all of creation. Whether one does it to prepare for death, or to make earth more like heaven, or to deepen one's sense of meaning, the task itself leads into religious concerns. Hillman goes on to say that without the soul connection to the Spirit, the richness of meaning is not possible. The following dream depicts my spiritual hunger:

WHY THE CUSTODIAN LOSES HEART

> The church in this dream is empty. I am outside it sweeping the twigs and leaves and debris off the walks and decks that surround it. I think about the job of custodian, and I think that whoever has that job now is not doing it as well as it could be done. I think that doing it properly would mean keeping busy at it all the time, finding things

to do that would enhance and improve the church. By my sweeping I am trying to show the custodian that his performance could be better. The church is enormous, made of gray stone, and the amount of area to sweep seems endless. I can see why the custodian loses heart.

Comments

If the custodian has no purpose other than to keep sweeping, then of course he loses heart. So do I. The endless attention to trash is disheartening. We need to go *inside* the church. The Spirit is inside the church. In order to take heart again, I need to serve the Spirit that dwells inside the church rather than the habit of tidiness that dwells outside. When I lose sight of this truth, I dry up and become miserable.

WHY THE CUSTODIAN LOSES HEART came several years before I began gathering up this material for presentation. The four months between it and THE CENTRAL INK DREAM were spent in a milestone event in my life: leaving the place I had lived all my life for a new home twenty five hundred miles away, chosen especially because it had spoken to me as a *sacred* place, a place that would enhance the inner work I had wanted to do for so long.

CHAPTER 5

Preservation

PRESERVING THE DIRT ON THE FLOOR

Now I am on my knees with a big paintbrush, applying a coat of clear preservative to a floor made of beautiful red rectangular tiles about 3" × 6". Suddenly I realize that I forgot to sweep the floor first. I am almost halfway finished, and I've been sealing in all the bits of dust and debris that have accumulated. I am overcome by dismay.

Associations

PRESERVATIVE: the written work that preserves these images. My journal is a long series of binders that contain not only the gold but all the tailings as well, all the debris of daily life: events, gossip, thoughts, dreams, drafts of poems, everything. When I look at all these volumes lined up, preserved in binder after binder, I am "overcome by dismay". How will it be possible to locate and extract the material for this book?

RED RECTANGULAR TILES: like the distinctive tile roof on the house where I raised my children. In the dream, those flat red roof tiles are now the floor. What was above is now below, as it says in ancient wisdom text, the Emerald Tablet, attributed to Hermes Trismegistus. I tentatively interpret this to mean (among other things) that when one approaches the divine as it speaks through the imagination, the divinity responds, which allows what was above to become the supporting floor below.

Much later, I will come to see that these words of wisdom also urge people to work toward making manifest what is sacred, a difficult task because of all the dirt and debris and mess and strife associated with earthly creations. Winnowing out the relevant images from the enormity of my journal is no small feat.

FLOOR: The support, the structural underpinning. There are broken floorboards, slippery floors, dance floors, etc., in my dreams. Here I am preserving the floor. Everything in one's past could be considered a part of the floor of the present. That I am preserving the debris rather than prettying it all up should please me, not dismay me. The temptation to make it all look good is hard to resist.

AGAIN THE DEBRIS: the detritus; the mess that's just there, forevermore. In dream work there is always something left over, an image that you don't understand, scraps that don't fit into whatever structure you devise to contain it. Preserving it instead of presuming to throw it away allows something else to come of it in time. If your dream work is being supervised by an expert, someone like a Jungian analyst, you will learn a great deal more about the images and their relevance to your situation than I will ever know. Perhaps your floors will be tidier.

DISMAY: Whenever I read through my writing or look at my visual art, I am dismayed by the disparity between the vision and its poor representation, as well as by the sheer mass of mess. But the fact that I feel dismay is no indication that I should abandon the project because it isn't going to be perfect.

CHAPTER 6

Important Instructions

LEARNING HOW TO BACK OUT

In this dream I have arranged for help cleaning all the houses I have ever lived in, as though I were still responsible for them. The housecleaner will need a ride to each place. I am getting instructions about where to park at each house, and especially how to back out of the parking area.

Associations

HELP: Someone else is going to help clean up the trash connected with my past. I don't have to do it all; I can allow someone to help me, a therapist, perhaps. I am only responsible for transporting the housecleaner or the therapist to the work site and for being able to back out properly.

At the time of this dream I had in fact begun to work with a therapist, and giving him "a ride to the places of my past" showed some progress in my willingness to trust him. This was J, a therapist who was not a Jungian analyst but who was skilled at working with products of the imagination in a Jungian way.

Trusting one's therapist is not easy. When I began working with J, I knew it would not be profitable for me to present my most up-beat and charming aspect. Displaying my unattractive, neurotic qualities required time and practice, and it was harder than one would think.

ALL THE HOUSES I'VE EVER LIVED IN: These houses might be the aspects of my personality that have been solid enough over time for me to set down roots and gather possessions: all of my complexes, all the knots of thread to be unraveled.

"Being in the house of" someone is like being under the influence of that person or place and manifesting a particular set of characteristics. The setting in a dream can provide a clue about "where you're at" and what "stuff" or "baggage" you're burdened with when the dream occurs.

RESPONSIBLE: The old knots from the past cause us trouble in the present. If we are responsible for anything, it's for our own lives and how we live them. It behooves us to attend to the complexes that pull our strings from behind the scenes or else our right hand will have no idea what mischief our left hand is doing.

BACKING OUT: The backing out is important. Getting stuck in one of these old places could make it impossible to complete the project. I have to be able to look at the material without getting lost in it. This is not easy.

One technique I use over and over again in this kind of writing is backing a little way out from a blocked place to where I can look at it and then writing a detailed account in my journal. First I close my eyes and breathe a few times. I murmur to myself, "Stuck. Stuck." Then I wait. What images cluster in this place? What words come? Sometimes imaginal people pop up and tell me things.

Anyone doing inner work will notice something that we all experience but most of us don't understand: feeling stuck in a mood or a behavior we'd like to get out of but can't. The technique of *backing out* is one of the most useful ways of dealing with this problem that I've found. Looking at and describing the mood or behavior as though from a bit of distance, even seeing oneself in third person, as from the point of view of a disinterested but helpful observer, makes it easier.

The next dream is even more promising. The man is fully present and enjoying himself. I have a wooded area with birds to share with the public. There's dirt on the floor, but it seems to belong there.

THE PUBLIC IS ABOUT TO ARRIVE

My house and grounds are being made open to the public. One of the attractions is a wooded area thronging with different species of birds. I can't name them, but when I get a good view of one through binoculars, I call out its description, "bright yellow body, black wings, black cowl, size of a crow, beak like a crow."

My baby grandson is here playing. He has gotten out all kinds of small objects, and now the floor is strewn with them. He asks me to play with him.

Down on the floor with the baby I notice that there's a layer of dirt like fine dry soil nearly an inch thick. The indoors and the outdoors have no clear dividing line, no wall separating them.

The people will be arriving soon. I ask Vance which he would rather do, go to the store for me or sweep up the dirt on the floor. He seems to be enjoying himself right here, and I suspect he's not going to do either one.

Associations

HOUSE AND GROUNDS OPEN TO THE PUBLIC: "Where I live" is about to be presented to the public. People will see my woods with all the birds.

The image of a woods often represents a place of spiritual concentration and introversion, of unconsciousness, while birds, being winged creatures, represent thoughts or spiritual beings. Thus a woods with birds on display to the public could be a reference to this project with its exploration of dream material brought out of the woods into the light of day and the variety of spirits inhabiting this coming-into-consciousness realm.

CROW: The crow-like bird with the bright yellow body is one of a number of bird images I've dreamed about. In one dream "*a crow flies right through a brick wall toward me. It is wearing a black beret, and we communicate by exchanging meaningful glances. I take it to a restaurant to feed it delicacies.*"

The present crow with its cowl and the earlier one with its beret seem to wear different hats for different occasions.

The image of the crow is also associated mythologically with the darkness, suffering and death that bring forth Asklepios, the Healer, child of the Sun God and the Crow Maiden. This image links the blackness of suffering with the gold of healing, and both are suggested by the yellow and black bird in this dream.

Never assume that you will negotiate a journey through your complexes without intense suffering. It is the suffering itself that brings forth the healing image, the Asklepios. The yellow parts of the crow give you hope for the gold that comes as the journey's reward.

NO WALL SEPARATING INDOORS FROM OUTDOORS: In the earlier dream about public presentation and the search for spirits, there was a Dutch door implying a partial opening. Here the wall itself is gone. The dirt suggests the *prima materia*, that unlovely stuff that alchemists of the imagination transform into gold.

BABY GRANDSON: My first grandchild, born on Christmas day. A child born in mid-winter symbolizes hope for new life coming out of the dark and cold, hope for a resurrection, just what one needs in the pit of depression.

PLAY AND ENJOYMENT: Both of the masculine elements, the baby and Vance, are enjoying themselves. This work must be done as play. Later dreams will make this more clear.

CHAPTER 7

What Comes of Working in the Trash

BRINGING BACK BURIED JEWELS

Now I am acting as a disinterested party to help a woman do something that she can't manage on her own. My work includes separating out bits of debris from her food so that she doesn't eat it and get sick. I separate out four blue beads from the food on her plate. The holes in the beads are encrusted with dirt, as though they had been buried. I am supposed to bring them back with me, and indeed my fingers are closed tight around them as I awaken from the dream.

Associations

DISINTERESTED PARTY: Now I am the helper. My ego, or center of consciousness, is performing the task that's most appropriate for it.

FOOD: Swallowing the food without separating out the debris would make a person sick. I have no doubt swallowed a lot of crud in my day, being unable to differentiate what nourishes from what sickens.

SEPARATING: In the myth of Eros and Psyche, one of Psyche's tasks was to separate. The reward for having done so was the reunion with Eros. Is that not what anyone in the dark pit of depression and creative blockage hopes for?

BURIED: Spiritual treasures are unearthed in the process of separating debris from nourishing food. My journals are like an enormous mine: the gold is there, but I have to separate it from the tailings.

FOUR BLUE BEADS: The number four is associated with wholeness and thus healing in the images of square, cube, cross, and the four points of the compass. Blue is the color of spirituality; jewels symbolize spiritual truths. Awakening from this dream, I am holding something of great value. Here, truly, I seem to be bringing forth what is within. It is palpable in my hand as I wake up.

PART 2

Traveling Zigzag

CHAPTER 8

Cars

When you don't know where you're going, it doesn't matter where you start. It took a while for me to figure this out, all the time trying to determine the theme for this next section, only to have the theme slip away as dream followed dream and images tangled together. What finally shaped up was a collection of dreams about cars and various other matters, starting with an orientation dream, and then moving back and forth through confusion, much like the actual dream work process itself.

An orientation dream is like a beacon shining through the fog of everyday life. My CENTRAL INK dream is an orientation dream. It tells me something about my center and about both where I'm coming from and where I'm going. The following is another such dream:

THE RED CAR AND THE CITY ON THE HILL

> I'm in a large parking lot where there is only one car. It's a compact car, red. I get in and start the engine. Now I see that the seat belt doesn't have a buckle. It has two straps just alike, like two right halves but no left. I get out to go indoors and report this defect, leaving my purse on the seat and the engine running. I'm also going to report that

there is only the one car out here, although it was understood that there were going to be enough cars for everybody. I look around to make sure there's nobody waiting to make off with the car I've already claimed.

Inside the building I catch a glimpse of the Director of the Writer's Center and think that the Center has really come up in the world. This place is not only higher but also more handsome than its old digs at the college.

Now I'm back in the parking lot going to the car. This building and lot are high on a hill, but across the street is an even higher, steeper hill. I watch in amazement as a car drives down that hill on a rudimentary black road that looks more like a coalfield than a street. At the top of this hill, high above me, a city is being built, big buildings, like the center section of a major city.

Now I am inside a building where there are other people. It has the atmosphere of a clinic, though it doesn't seem medical. I notice a man watching me with bold eyes, and even though he is not my type, I know that I will accept him as a sexual partner. "What the hell?" I think. My usual inhibitions about disease and incompatibility, my hesitations about my aging body, are not in effect.

But first I am working my way into a garment that pulls on over the head without any buttons or zippers. It's tight going on, and getting my elbows through takes a struggle, with me trying not to rip anything. The garment is a long-sleeved fitted red dress, seamless from throat to feet. Once I get it on, it should fit perfectly, but I don't expect it to be very becoming.

Associations

ONE RED CAR: The car is there just for me, and I take it. Maybe it's like this work, a vehicle for me alone; neither another person nor another car is anywhere in sight. Because it's red and small, it looks like the first car

I ever bought for myself, a little red Subaru. Like the work, the car is modest but mine.

Some interpreters of dreams think of the image of a car as an instrument of the ego. Ideally the ego would be the conscious servant of the core self, as a human might ideally be the conscious servant of the divinity. But most of our egos are contaminated by the influence of the most powerful of our other psychological parts, just as we servants of the divine are influenced by other people, by the groups we belong to, by thoughts and images, and by such entities as governments and corporations whose interests are entirely secular. If we think of our entire person as an association with a number of members, like the United Nations, perhaps, each of whom has special interests, then the block that most often gets its way is like an inner Security Council. The vehicle we usually drive, then, is a representation of the wishes of those who control things, and the ego is taken over, or perhaps complicit.

Since red is the color of energy and desire, for me to be claiming a red car in this dream could indicate that my ego's outward efforts and my inner flow of energy have a common goal. And because of the location of the dream, this little red car does not seem to represent my usual power block, which consists of parents with conflicting agendas, temperamental partners, various admonitions from society, and howling children. This is *not* my father's Oldsmobile!

Certainly the use of the word "vehicle" to mean a medium for expression cannot be overlooked here. This book is such a vehicle and is perhaps alluded to by the dream.

UNUSABLE SAFETY BELT: In this new car, this new way of moving through life and expressing myself, I cannot be as concerned about safety as I have been in the past. Being that careful is no longer appropriate. It's time to unbuckle.

ENGINE RUNNING, PURSE ON THE SEAT: Already I'm learning! In waking life I would no doubt turn off the engine, lock the car and clutch my purse against me, look both ways (in the empty lot) and proceed cautiously into the building, careful not to slip on ice or mud or banana peels. And in waking life at least some of those precautions would be appropriate. But in this metaphor I'm maintaining the energy flow in the vehicle and even leaving my purse, which is another image of the life force, since it contains another form of energy: money. Thus I am not taking energy away from the vehicle when I go inside to fuss-budget about the seat belt and the dearth of vehicles for other people. In a perfect dream I wouldn't fuss-budget, but old habits die slowly, with many harrowing deathbed scenes followed by miraculous remissions, and that's if they have the good grace to die at all.

THE WRITERS' CENTER: The Director of the Writers' Center is no longer an active acquaintance with whom I work on literary events. His appearances in my dream life are probably about his title, Director. The Writers' Center, of course, is a metaphor for my own center, like the Central Ink building.

This fleeting image places the dream. I am in the area of my own central core.

CITY BEING BUILT: On a high hill buildings are going up. There are many images of one's central core, the divine image within. The city is one of them. The city high on the hill might represent something greater than my own small reflection of godliness. Its position suggests another, more elevated, level that approaches the heavenly city I sang about in Sunday School as a child. It takes a community to build a city. A single person cannot do it. I am making what efforts I can to inhabit my center and live my destiny, but I am only an assistant to whatever emissary of the deity takes an interest in me, and in this dream only a spectator. For an inner city to be built, the members of my personal committee have to act in enough agreement to get something done.

Some time ago in a dream, I gazed through the window of a bus terminal downtown in a grubby city. Across the street was a building with a beautifully lighted window over which was a sign that read: PROMISED LAND. This city on the hill seems like a similar glimpse of where I'm trying to go.

SEXUAL PARTNER: Here too my usual carefulness is not in effect. I don't know who this man is, but he's some manifestation of my *inner* man, the multi-faceted image of masculinity (cohesive thrust?) that I carry within. He has qualities that I lack in my conscious life, and in this manifestation the quality is bold eyes. By accepting him I accept the bold eyes I need to carry through toward my goal. With those eyes perhaps I can pay attention and see through what seems obscure.

The setting is one of those places where we go to get something we need. We line up and talk with people behind desks. The implication is that I need what this man has.

RED DRESS: In *Daughter of Hearts, Daughter of Clubs* the Tight Fist tore a red dress off Carrie. It happened just that way in my own life, and this event, along with the family situation that made the event possible, greatly impeded my feminine presentation. But in this dream I am sliding the red dress back on, and it's fitting perfectly. In the metaphorical sense, wearing a dress that displays my feminine energy and desire is exactly right.

Will it be becoming? Who knows? Being myself is quite different from being concerned with whether others like me. Maybe they will—and maybe they won't.

We don't get to choose who we are. We don't get to be who we want to be, TV commercials and self-help manuals notwithstanding. We can either be who we are, at whatever stage of development, or we can be false.

The following dream about performance is one of the first dreams I had upon arriving at my new home, and it ushered in a several-year period of becoming aware of and acquainted with the imagined little girl who is something like I once was:

THE PERFORMANCE CAR DREAM

> In this dream I have just finished graduate school. One of the perks that came with the degree is the use of a huge, expensive, performance car, a custom-made vehicle the

size of a van with fenders like animal haunches. I am now on my way home, driving this car.

Along the way I stop to pick up a baby who is supposed to ride along with me. I park in a driveway made of soft black earth like potting soil inlaid with a mosaic of wood chips. Walking on the soil-and-chips path, I skirt a muddy area and go indoors to get the baby, a little girl of about ten months. The mother hands her over without a qualm.

Now I am out on the highway. There is no baby seat in the car, and the child is riding unbuckled and unsafe on my lap. A lot of people are standing around in the road. Driving involves dodging so many children that it seems like an obstacle course. Controlling this car is not easy, especially under these conditions. It is very large, and it has so much power that any pressure on the gas pedal results in an almost uncontrollable surge. In one place I have to stop completely to avoid running down a little boy in the middle of the road. I open my window to call out for someone to get him out of the way.

Now I realize that the baby is wearing only a sun suit and has no change of clothing, that the mother sent no diapers with her. I think of turning back to get what I need to care for the little one. But the obstacles have been so tiring and time-consuming that I simply haven't the heart to go through them all again.

Associations

BIG PERFORMANCE CAR: This car does not actually belong to me; I only have the use of it. Like a rental car, it may help me get where I am going, but it isn't really what suits me. Nevertheless I did the work necessary to earn my degree, and so I accept it as a perk and get in. Such a perk carries a price, and that price is the expectation that its driver will achieve acclaim to feed back to the Alma Mater so that the school can shine in the reflected glory of its esteemed graduates. The school I attended shone brightly in this way.

FINISHED GRADUATE SCHOOL: This suggests the end of the two years I actually did spend earning my master's degree. But it would be a mistake to overlook the harking back of this event to my early childhood as well. Both were periods of learning new ways to produce and to perform, and during both the message was stressed that I was expected to do so in a far better than average way.

"Alma Mater" means "nourishing mother," but mothers who push their children into too-early performance and feed on the tidbits of acclaim therefrom are not actually being nourishing, no matter how delightful they are or how much attention they lavish on their offspring. I had such a mother (as well as such an Alma Mater), and the experience of growing up in that environment hampers me whenever my productivity as an adult comes into question. The feelings of the child still alive in me rebel against having to perform for praise, and I find myself immobilized between the urging mother and the recalcitrant child.

GOING HOME: Home, here, of course, is not the literal place I live in. "Home" in dream language is more likely to mean a return to who you are under all the education and cultural expectations and societal polish. It's more like the inner, sacred home, the Promised Land.

Still, it took the attempts to manage the big Performance car to bring me to the place where the spiritual practice of my soul work could begin. It carried me part of the way. If it were not for all the past work I have done, writing poems and stories, I would not be able to respond to the call to persist with the present work. Even the most unlikely vehicle can move you along on your journey.

People journey "home" by different routes. In this dream the Performance car took me first to the place where I had to meet my imagined child and bring her along.

SOFT BLACK EARTH: The driveway and path are more like a garden site, fresh earth, a place for planting, not driving. Leaving the monster of a vehicle behind, I continue on foot. In such an area one would expect things to start growing. The alchemists talked about the *prima materia* as the beginning, the soil that, when worked, produced fruit, or gold, or the opus.

The "black earth" may also refer to the complicated image of Melanchthon, a German religious reformer of the early sixteenth century, whose name is the Greek rendering of the German "Schwarzerd" which means "black earth." Before my first child was born, the family's nickname for the baby-to-be was Melanchthon, a name seemingly pulled out of the air. While in graduate school, I wrote a story called "Melanchton and the Process Server"[4] about a young woman's attempts to keep her newborn babies from disappearing. The appearance of black earth here indicates that the child is in danger of being lost but can be saved through working the soil.

WOOD-CHIP MOSAIC: The inlay of a wood-chip mosaic implies a design already overlaid on the *prima materia* of the soil. This corresponds to the baby's age, "about ten months," when a child has received not only whatever innate package she was born with but also the pattern imposed by parental care.

AVOIDING THE MUD: I skirt, for the time being, the place where I'm going to get muddy, the place of shame and embarrassment, where you slip and come up with dirt all over you. Perhaps I sense (correctly!) that once in the mud hole, I will wallow there for what seems forever, where movement is measured in the few inches one travels to find a fresh place to wallow, like shifting in the bed to find a cool spot. Here, progress is nothing more than finding fresh mud. It's moving out of wallowed mud into fresh mud on the way Home, which seems unattainable. No wonder I skirt it. Don't we all, as long as we can?

4. "Melanchthon and the Process Server" was published in *New Fiction From Indiana*.

MOTHER: The mother, here, bears noticing. She hands a young baby over to ride in the performance car without a qualm, where a more nourishing mother might well hesitate. And she does not provide a well-stocked diaper bag.

The reference for "diapers" led into the relics of my childhood, where I found the childcare manual my old-fashioned parents read (and followed). In it was such advice as:

- Feed regularly, by the clock, not by impulse.
- Young infants should lie quietly in bed till strong enough to sit alone and play.
- Break the habit of thumb sucking, no matter what effort it costs you.
- Any baby over 3 months old may be trained to evacuate the bowels.

My parents were not unusual in following these dismal instructions. The experts advised, the parents complied, just as they do today. Years later we all try to overcome the damage. In my case, learning so early to perform on the potty and do without diapers set me up for a wretched Performance complex. My family thought I was wonderful, bragged about me and laid on the praise, since I was both weaned and able to use the potty by the time I was six months old. (See *Being Weaned* below.)

TRYING TO CONTROL THE PERFORMANCE CAR: High-powered performance cars are not okay for children. Babies are new beings, just getting started, needing a nurturing environment, not a demanding one. In artistic creation, new projects are often seen as the artist's children and dreamed of as babies. They have to be protected from the demands of the outer world, the editors, critics, and gallery owners, and even more protected from the inner representations of those self-serving audiences, in order to be nourished into growth.

STOPPING THE CAR: I come to a stop to protect a little boy who may well represent my own undeveloped "masculine" qualities. To continue would endanger him and the other children nearby, as well as the un-provided-for baby girl on my lap.

The stop may refer to the halt I came to in writing. My ability to move in the performance vehicle came to an end at that point.

The following dream and its related story lead a long way from THE PERFORMANCE CAR DREAM and the baby girl I have taken responsibility for, but it seems so relevant to the issues that I will include it here, before getting back to the child and her wishes. The dream is:

BEING WEANED

> Scene 1: I have given birth to twins, one of whom is a bear cub. I'm delighted with the cub and its heavy fur, and although I wonder if it's normal for a human to give birth to a bear, I enjoy taking the cub with me everywhere I go.
>
> Scene 2: I am being weaned. Every time I do without what I want, I'm rewarded. A cup full of change is set out for me. The cups are placed farther and farther away from me in all directions. I begin to suspect that I'm being taken farther and farther away from myself. At that point I start noticing how much money is in the cups. It's mostly pennies with just enough bigger coins to sweeten the pot.

The story that follows came to me as a fantasy that I experienced when I allowed myself to re-imagine the first scene of this dream. Although I did not expressly deal with Scene 2, writing the fantasy had the effect of showing me how to get back to myself after having been weaned away at a very early age.

The Other Real World[5]

When the new mother had healed enough from the shock of the double birth to take the baby home from the hospital, she took the bear cub as well. They urged her to put him in a zoo, where a mother bear might adopt and nurse him. But the cub was her flesh and blood, just as the baby was, and she was going to keep him, difficult as it might be.

She dressed them like twins for a week or so: little shirts and diapers, knit gowns, bibs. But the cub had his own garment: soft bear fur was all he needed. So the baby got the wardrobe and the cub was allowed to be a bear.

She continued to care for them equally, however, and they both thrived. They slept in the room where she worked sewing shirt seams for the factory, the cub in a warm den under the baby's crib. As the months went by and the twins grew, the bars between them posed less and less of a barrier. First the bear learned to climb *in*, then the baby to climb *out*. Inside the crib they played with the rattles, the stuffed animals, the musical mobile that swung from the headboard. On the floor they played with the ball, the blocks, the rocking horse, and the chicken that clucked when dragged across the floor, all to the background hum of their mother's sewing machine.

One toy, however, that the bear failed to enjoy was the tall mirror attached to the door. The baby would look in it and smile, enchanted by her own image, while the bear smelled it and batted it with a paw, treating it like an inanimate piece of glass and growling to draw the baby's attention back to where he felt it belonged, on him.

"How fortunate!" thought their mother. "Most little girls have no bear twin to remind them that the mirror isn't everything." And she took the big mirror away and substituted a small one.

The mother had an old fur coat of *her* mother's, shabby and disreputable, that she wore sometimes when she walked alone in the woods near her home. A coat to withdraw in, one for animal warmth, not human gaze. She pushed the twins into the woods in a double stroller. The

5. "The Other Real World" was published in *Flying Island*.

path was just wide enough to accommodate them, no wider. No one else was ever there. The woman and her children had the whole woods to themselves.

"How fortunate!" she thought again. Taking the children in the stroller through the neighborhood had never been a rewarding experience. In the neighborhood they were on display, but in the woods they could be themselves.

The entrance to the woods was always the same, through a gate in the stone wall that encircled the small wild area in the midst of suburban sprawl, a little section of green saved from the endless shopping malls and tract houses. But once inside, the woman noticed that the path was different from one day to the next. At first she attributed the changes to her unfamiliarity with the woods, but after enough walks, she realized that something else was involved, something she couldn't quite grasp.

For one thing, the woods grew larger. The path that took half an hour to travel the first time now stretched far enough to take half a day. "And I'm not walking any more slowly," she thought.

The food she found in the woods changed too. On the first day she ate two ripe thimbleberries, and that was all she found. But as the walk got longer, more food appeared. There was no need to bring a lunch. The picnic was already there, spread out for the taking. Not just thimbleberries, though the bear liked them a lot, but fresh fish as well, cooking in a small firepit just off the path, or a hot round loaf of bread which she could smell baking in a hive-shaped oven. There was milk for the children and wine for herself, cooling in jugs submerged in a shaded stream.

At first she did not take any, thinking the food belonged to someone else. But one day she had neglected to eat breakfast and was very hungry. The bread smelled wonderful. "Just a bite," she thought, and helped herself. One bite led to another, as usual, and of course she had to give some to her daughter and the bear. Soon the loaf was gone.

"I can't believe I really did that," she said to herself, ashamed. "I've become a thief." But by then the hive-shaped oven was once again redolent of baking bread. Another loaf had taken the place of what she'd eaten.

"This is a miracle," she thought. "If I hadn't given birth to the bear as well as the child, I'd have never found this place where food replenishes itself as soon as it's consumed. I'd have stayed home or gone to the mall. I'd have been just another vain, unhappy consumer, and so would my daughter."

She continued to spend her spare time in the woods. As she did so, the woods continued to grow. At last she realized that the woods was no longer just a token scrap of green within the sprawl of civilization. It now covered enough territory so that the suburb was small by comparison. "This is more like it," she thought.

But one evening a member of the Community Council came knocking at her door. He was inquiring of all citizens how they spent their time. "What contribution are you making to society?" he asked. He left a questionnaire.

She pondered the question as she sewed that night. What contribution *was* she making? Wasn't she spending her time selfishly? Doing what she pleased instead of what she ought to do? She was avoiding the trap of the mirror and the shopping mall, but what was she doing for society?

The next day she stayed home from the woods and filled out the questionnaire. The twins played in the kitchen. The little girl whined to be taken out, and the cub left droppings on the floor. But that was the price she'd have to pay, she thought, to be a better citizen. When her phone rang and she was asked to help support a Community Council candidate, one who promised to be more responsive to the citizens' wishes, she involved herself in the campaign.

It was exciting to feel she could make a difference. Being part of the group made her feel useful. Yes, she had to spend more time at the shopping mall, for that's where Campaign Headquarters was located. And yes, she had to spend more time at the mirror, because looks counted at the mall. But it was the campaign that mattered, and she could afford to make some sacrifices for that.

She took the child with her to play with the other children while she worked. The bear, of course, had to stay at home. He didn't behave well alone, and she had to build him a pen.

"That's the price you have to pay for good government," she thought. For citizen involvement. It was too bad. She missed the woods, the happiness of the bear, but what right did she have to these luxuries when the society was going to hell? How could she abdicate her responsibilities as a citizen? How could she leave the town in a mess for her child to grow up in?

She did worry about the bear. It paced its pen and growled when she approached to toss in its food. She promised herself that she would do better by the bear as soon as she had more time.

Her candidate won. The victory party lasted late. Wine was drunk. The thought did come to her, as she was sipping a glass of it, that the wine from the jugs in the stream in the woods had been better. Much better. And it hadn't left her hung over.

But such thoughts were elitist, weren't they? What right did she have to fine wine?

The new Community Council settled in. Meetings were held. Bills were passed. Citizens wrote letters to the editor. The business of the suburb went on. Yes, there were changes. Permission to build the ten-story hotel was refused. But when the developers scaled down their project and a compromise was reached, a five-story office building went up on a slightly larger site.

There was time now for the woman to go back to the woods. She could spend a little time strolling on the ever-changing path, feasting on the picnic there for the taking. But her daughter whined at the prospect. "I want to go to the mall," she cried. "My friends all go to the mall." "Already the girl says this, so young!" thought the mother. And the bear had become so dangerous that she dared not let him out of his pen. He might go on a rampage and maul somebody. She would have to walk in the woods alone.

The gate was just as she remembered it. She entered. Trees arched over the path. The peace of the woods embraced her. She walked, rejoicing, her shabby fur coat wrapped around her. She wondered what she would find to eat. She walked on. But after twenty minutes she was back at the gate. The woods had shrunk. She had found nothing at all to eat.

"Could I have been mistaken about the woods?" she asked herself. She stood there by the entrance, hating to leave, feeling deprived. Her gaze fell on a thicket. One ripe thimbleberry hung crimson on a branch. "No," she thought, "I wasn't mistaken. This is real, as real as anything there is." She popped the thimbleberry into her mouth and fitted it over the end of her tongue like a cap.

But the woods had definitely shrunk. She hadn't spent half an hour on the path before coming to the end of it. The suburb had squeezed it smaller and smaller. What a pity! She would have to speak to the Community Council. After all she'd done for her candidate, he ought to represent her and take her concerns seriously.

He spoke kindly to her. "There, there," he said. "I'm sorry you're so upset. But this is the real world. Progress is progress."

She understood. Nothing could be done. The Community Council would be no help. The real world was the real world, and progress was progress. The candidate was helpless against it. Her spirits were very low.

That night before going to sleep, she prayed for the first time since childhood. "I need help," she prayed. "Somebody help me, please." She didn't really believe in God anymore, but she needed to pray anyway. "What can I do?" she asked. "My daughter is lost to the shopping mall, the bear is too dangerous to let out of his pen, and the woods have shrunk alarmingly."

After a time she awoke, thinking that she'd been dreaming she was standing near the stream in the woods. The jugs were cooling in the water. The hive-shaped oven sent forth its aroma. The fresh fish sizzled on a circle of firestones. Someone was standing nearby holding a high-powered flashlight, the beam of which penetrated the darkness of the woods. She saw a pattern of stones that looked like the foundation of some kind of structure, but she couldn't tell what it was. Then she heard a voice. "The real world is the real world," it said. She glared angrily. She'd heard those words before. But the voice spoke again. "All you have to do is come here," it said. "The forest is real, but only if you come."

She felt the hairs on her arms lift. She also felt dizzy from the view, the view she was glimpsing of a real world dependent upon her attendance. If she did *not* go there, it would disappear, perhaps disappear entirely.

But so would the shopping mall. If nobody went there, it would cease to be real.

But what about her daughter, she wondered.

"Your daughter will find the woods herself some day," came the answer. "If she's so inclined."

"And the bear?"

"Open the pen." This voice from within sounded authentic. It certainly carried more authority than the voice of her candidate, who could come up with nothing better than "There, there," and "Progress is progress." She opened the pen.

The bear shambled out and disappeared into the woods. In her future visits she would sometimes hear him crash around in the underbrush, and once she saw him raking thimbleberries off the stalks.

Again she attended the woods daily, only now she did more than stroll. Sometimes she saw the foundation of the structure again, where new stones appeared from time to time. Sometimes she sensed the presence of someone else, and was able to converse with the voice she had heard. There was always food nearby.

When the call came for her to return to the campaign, her answer was ready. "No," she said. "That's not the best use of my time."

"What about your contribution?" This question again, the one that had led to her losses.

"I am making a different contribution," she said. "The real world is the real world." Far too many people already were making the candidate's world real; her contribution was to attend to the other world she had found.

The candidate was angry and critical. She was no longer useful to him and therefore would be disregarded.

But she'd already paid the price of leaving the woods. This time she would pay the price of finding it again. Every choice requires a sacrifice.

Months and years went by. The woman continued her attendance to the woods. The stone structure grew higher. Her old coat grew more and more shabby.

The home she made for her daughter kept her involved with the community as well. People continued to ask her to make a contribution, to back a candidate or work on a committee. Occasionally she found community work that did not violate her commitment to what she began to call "silvaculture" for lack of a better term. This put her in contact with others interested in things besides the mirror and the shopping mall. She made connections.

One day the daughter of her old Community Council candidate came to visit. What she wanted was not clear at first. "I've heard about you," the girl said. "I think you're the one who can help me." They talked a little, about one thing and another, and then she got down to the point. "I dreamed I gave birth to twins," she said. "And one of them was a seal pup."

The woman nodded. "Yes," she said. "Maybe I can help you. I'll meet you tomorrow and we'll talk. But there's a special place you'll have to go," she said. "I can show you the entrance, but you'll have to go inside alone. We'll meet there tomorrow."

"Where?" asked the girl, eyeing the woman's berry-stained fingers. "In the woods?"

"No," answered the woman. "On the beach."

Returning to the issue of caring for the child so poorly while driving the Performance vehicle, I need to allow this child to speak for herself and to expand the cast of characters who act out my inner drama.

I have taken part in dream study groups for many years, both as a participant and as a facilitator. After a while it becomes noticeable that each person's dream life is as individual as his or her waking life. The cast of characters becomes known, the stage settings, the kinds of activity.

Dreams personify different aspects of ourselves. When I dream about my mother or my father, I am seeing the images of my parents that I still carry as parts of myself, both nurturing and hampering. The actual parents who raised me might not recognize themselves as they are portrayed herein. The child who is so prominent a character here is not the flesh-and-blood, living-and-breathing Marcia as she was at age four or six; but she has taken on a distinct personality and is alive in the same way a character in a book or play is alive.

THE CHILD STANDS UP FOR HERSELF

> A little girl is restrained in the back seat of my car. Her arms are held down and she is belted in tightly around the middle. "I want to stand up now," she says, and as I reach around from the driver's seat and unfasten her, she does so.

The Child, Mmmmm, Says:

I am the little girl in the car. My name is not Carrie. It's Mmmmm, pronounced "Mm" with the lips closed, not "Em" or "Um," and spelled with five mmmmm's, the first one large, the others small. Marcia tried to cut it down to three, which she said would look more graceful, and not fall off the corner of my pictures, and besides, she said, think of all those keystrokes she would save typing Mmm instead of Mmmmm. She tends to hoard time and energy, to squirrel it away in a hole in the ground. But it takes five mmmmm's to express who I am, and generosity about my expression is more important than gracefulness or frugality.

I am Mmmmm because I like to hum while I suck my thumb. Each hum makes a little tune five mmmmm's long. The middle goes up, like this: mm^{m}mm. The whole tune is as long as a breath. I take the thumb-guards off, suck for a while, then pop the guards back on before my mama catches me or worse still, my daddy.

I am also Mmmmm because I have to be careful what I say. Sometimes I say "mmmmm" before I answer a question to give myself time to consider all the ramifications. To get my story straight. If my story is crooked, I will be accused of violating the unities and the verities and everybody's thumbs will turn down.

With a story like mine it is hard to avoid violating the unities and the verities. Stories are like nuts, with the rich truthful meat contained in a shell of unity, piñons in little shells, coconuts in big ones. When you open the shell, there's the meat of the story, all shapely and singular, an almond or a hazelnut. But my story is not shapely like an almond. It is like the kernel of a hard-to-crack black walnut, shattered. First you have to dig up the nut where the squirrel has hidden it and drive your car over it to take off the green outer husk that stains your fingers if you touch it. Then you have to smash it with a sledgehammer to break open the deeply furrowed dark brown shell. No one has ever seen a black walnut kernel all in one piece, because by this time the kernel is broken up and the unities have been destroyed forever. The verities can still be discovered, however. You can gather up whatever little pieces are not squashed into the ground and bake a cake with them. When you taste the cake, you recognize the verity in what you have. This is what my story is like.

Lastly I am Mmmmm because I like good things to eat. Black walnut cake would be especially delicious.

Marcia Says:

My name is Marcia, given to me by my father, and derived from Mars, the Roman god of war. The cold planet. I house the chilly strife between my parents that resulted from their loyalties to families with different values and styles. Instead of cleaving to each other, each clung to the parental family to the very end, when my mother chose to be buried with her people in Mt. Pleasant Cemetery south of town and my father took a grave in Crown Hill, on the north side, where his great-grandfather had bought a block of plots when the cemetery was first created.

Family wars, even cold ones, like wars of state, consume vast amounts of wealth. Much of my birthright of talent and energy has been used up on the weaponry of defense, first by my parents who brought me up and finally by the inner parents and their hangers-on that I house to this day as psychological entities.

I do not state this to excuse myself for anything. Nor do I blame my parents. By almost any standards, they were good parents. We all have the circumstances of our lives to deal with, whatever they are, for better or worse. But we can assume responsibility only when we know what the circumstances are.

My desire to do soul work arose when I was in my late thirties. My first husband and I were separating, and I was about to go off to graduate school. C. G. Jung's *Memories, Dreams and Reflections* and *Man and His Symbols* made such an impression on me that I struggled through the big black volumes of Jung's *Collected Works* during the two years I attended classes, studied, wrote fiction, worked as a secretary in the Admissions Office and made a home for my two young daughters. Much of Jung's writing was abstruse and incomprehensible, filled with foreign terminology and references to ancient texts that I had barely heard of, but even the *Collected Works* could not put me off.

Writing fiction and poetry had been the beginning of it. Occasionally images would come to me of such interest and vividness that I wrote poems or stories to discover what they wanted or where they would go. This way I learned that there was a great deal about myself that I didn't know, and that the parts I didn't know seemed to be running things.

There were no Jungian analysts or therapists that I knew of either in my home town or where I went to graduate school, and even if there had been, I would not have considered spending money on a personal luxury like soul work. So instead, I continued writing stories and poems, and I began keeping a journal that included my dreams.

Not until years later, when Vance retired and we moved to the Pacific Northwest, where Jungians flourish like salal on the hillsides, was I able to realize my big dream of doing this work with the help of a therapist who also felt their influence.

My ability to write fiction and poetry lessened as though the inner need for self-expression had found a wider opening. I experienced this with grief and shame, for I had a lot invested in being a writer whose work found an audience. Inner work, by nature, is private, without the reward of audience feedback. It does not have the same approval from society that producing entertainment or even art has, and my inner "committee" called me to task with such accusations as "navel-gazing" and "self-indulgence." What I was now doing had no value in the literary marketplace. Nevertheless it was what I wanted, and all the stories and poems I had written before fed into that desire. When I began, I hoped that my soul work would aid me in my other writing, but after a while I realized, with considerable chagrin, that it was the other way around: my other writing contributed to my soul work. Instead of a career in writing, I had a calling, a spiritual practice.

If I had known what to look for, I might have discovered this before spending the time, money and energy it took to earn a graduate degree. This kind of expenditure is approved when it leads to a career producing a commodity like saleable fiction, but most people would consider it wasted if it only leads to soul work. I did not ask myself how I felt about a career; thus, I was unaware that "lit biz" would be so unattractive to me that my creative flow would shut down at the mere thought of it.

By "soul," I'm not talking about personal immortality. I simply mean the fourth part of the human being: the part that speaks through imagination. We attend to the needs of the *body* when we eat right, work out, maintain our physical selves and our physical world. We improve the *mind* when we study, think, and employ our reason. We take care of the *heart* when we love, feel deeply, value and prefer. But it is through the imagination of the *soul* that Creation continues its sacred work. When I teach imaginative writing exercises whose purpose is not to be made public but to develop and strengthen the imagination, I think of my class as one in "soul yoga."

I cannot know for sure that there is any overall meaning to life as a whole, any purpose, any interested deity. I struggle with these issues often. J, who has been my therapist and dream work guide since I began, points out that the meaning is in the struggle itself. My skeptical streak, my "Cold Fishy Eye" (see picture, next page) is very strong. I am not a believer. I am a seeker, a follower of images, looking, not for the Meaning of Life but for the meaning of *my* life as it is revealed to me, little by little.

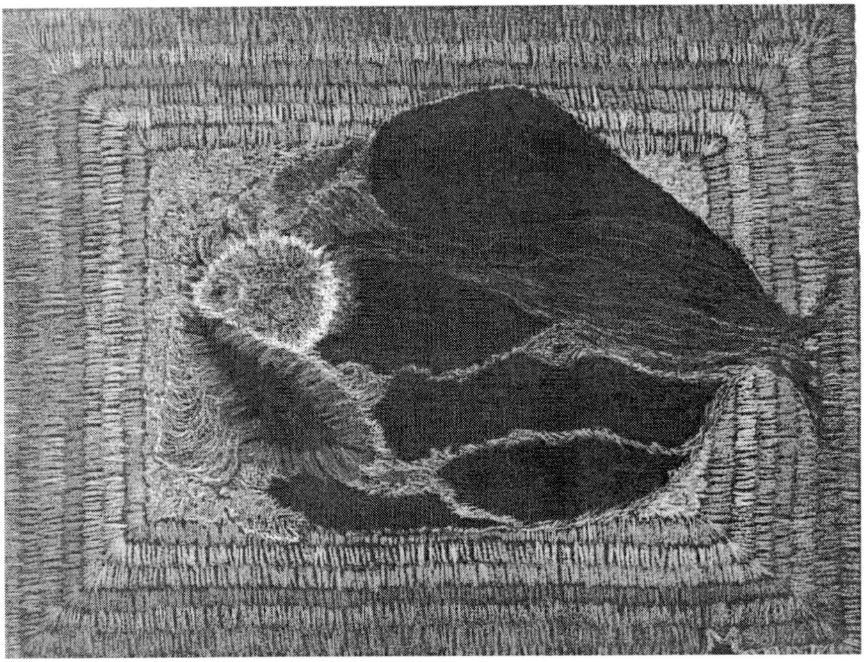

Cold Fishy Eye

CHAPTER 9

Escape

The next car dream deals with the Maintenance vehicle, the one prescribed by my father, like the rules of the Tight Fist of Clubs to govern Carrie's behavior.

GM CARS BEING RECALLED

> In the dream I have taken my car to a mechanic's shop and am talking with the man in charge while I wait. He asks something about my car, then tells me it is one of those being recalled by the manufacturer. This is not my Subaru; it's a GM car.
>
> We are standing outside the shop now. You can see a long way away, and in the distance there's a big fire with people moving around, looking like shadows against the flames. Every so often a great burst of flame surges upward, and you can tell that someone has added a drum of gasoline or other fuel. I am frightened and want to get my car and leave for fear that I will be burned. I imagine myself in the flames and wonder how long it takes to die that way.

Now we are inside the shop again talking about the car being recalled. He has done some paperwork and prepared a round wooden plaque with a street address carved into the wood underneath a design. He tells me that because of this address the car is definitely supposed to be recalled.

"But that's not my address," I answer. "That's where my aunt lives." I am completely confused.

Associations

GM CAR: My father worked for General Motors as a tool and die maker, and he always drove GM cars. This car really is "my father's Oldsmobile."

RECALLED: means both "remembered" and "returned because of defects." This is the vehicle I call *Maintenance* because it serves to preserve the status quo and keep me out of trouble. Like the *Performance* vehicle, it helped to get me here, and it has served its purpose.

FIRE: A symbol of passion, strong feeling, transformation of energy. I am afraid of it, afraid of being burned by it. What might happen to me if I let my life be directed more by passion and less by carefulness? Do I really want any transformation? The people who want transformation forget that you can just as easily become a frog as a prince.

AUNT'S ADDRESS: The aunt in question also drove Oldsmobiles. She stayed in the neighborhood and lived as my father would have liked me to live, following the family rules he lived by and passed on to me:

- Be dependable and punctual
- Don't carry on about things
- Don't run things into the ground
- Have a pleasant, polite attitude
- Don't get involved with people

- Don't spend money
- Don't borrow
- Don't lend
- Keep the lawn in order before you think about a flower bed
- Keep yourself clean and neat; avoid provocative clothing
- Hold to your schedule
- Bite off only what you can chew
- Finish what you start
- Expect nothing
- Avoid trouble
- NO FUNNY STUFF: no sex, no art, no spirituality
- Don't get all worked up
- ABOVE ALL: don't let anything happen to you

That aunt shares two escape strategies with me: food and library books. My great fear, like bag-lady fears and derelict-on-the-park-bench fears, is that I will turn out like this aunt, with nothing in my life but those escapes. "Where my aunt lives" is with food and books.

ESCAPE INTO BOOKS

> At first we all say, "Well, at least we'll always be able to get books," but then the supply dwindles and we realize that we can't count on this either.

Comments (Continued)

These dreams have in common the theme of escape. I noticed this and typed them together on a page to consider. Immediately some distressing physical feelings came over me: a gag reflex, as though something was trying to come up, and the feeling that tears were unable to burst through. I read through the dreams again, hoping to be enlightened as to the meaning of my distress. Instead, I felt the misery localize in two places, in the center of my forehead and in my chest near my heart. I began yawning, huge yawns, and I felt so cold that I was shivering.

Fortunately I had an appointment to see J, my therapist, later that day, and I took these dreams and my distress with me. I also took my fears that this manuscript was going to be impossible, that I could never keep going with it. I read J a little dialogue with another of my cast of inner characters, the Sick One, who is a grown up version of myself as a sick child and suspiciously like my aunt in her taste for escapes.

The Sick One appears here as the woman in BRINGING BACK BURIED JEWELS who needs to have the dirt separated from her food. Edward F. Edinger, in his book, *Anatomy of the Psyche*, described the alchemical operation called the *separatio* as having a cleansing function that helps to clean up one's attitudes that have been contaminated by unconscious complexes. As the "disinterested" party, then, I would be helping to conduct a scrutiny of my complexes, as Edinger recommends. The Sick One is not enthusiastic about this effort:

She says: "What's the use? Why so eager to engage this project? This trip's going to be grim, legs all tired, too heavy a load, plod-along, plod-along, muddy roads, flat tires, cars going dead."

She says: "You're not hearing me now but you will. I always manage to convince you that you're not going anywhere, that you're going to stay right here in the neighborhood, none of this far-to-go business, that where you live is right here with a library book and a sandwich."

J invited me to use the Magic Circle to help move the process along.

The Magic Circle came into existence at Mmmmm's behest when I was trying to imagine the life I led before the age of seven. I could slip into a slightly altered state rather easily, but the child part of me did not feel safe. She did not yet trust J to protect her. In her own inimitable way she told him that what she wanted was for him to make a Magic Circle around her where nothing bad could happen.

To my great surprise he did exactly that. He shoved his battered couches and sagging chairs and leaky pillows into a circle within which we sat cross-legged on the floor. He then smudged the circle with smoking sweet-grass and a large feather, calling down spiritual powers to protect us while we did this work. This roused my Cold Fishy Eye, and the Fist said, "No funny stuff," but Mmmmm decided that J didn't think this was mumbo-jumbo even if the Fist did, and that J would not dare to let anyone hurt her while the spirits he believed in were watching. Thus she was able to come forth and allow us to make her acquaintance. Even after many months had passed and the need to make Mmmmm safe had lessened, we continued to use the Magic Circle for any deep work that needed to be done.

On this particular day, when I reached J's office, I immediately felt physical sensations of bursting, of enormous inner turmoil. I was gasping for air and, listening to the audio tape later, I could hear that my voice was intense as I spoke aloud what I was experiencing.

The first image that came to me was of being on a boat that intended to pull away from the dock in a measured way but instead was being blown away, ripped away from the dock by a high wind, into the turmoil of a stormy sea. "The Spirit," murmured J, from the edge of the Magic Circle. "Being blown by the wind of Spirit."

I felt battered and buffeted. Torn. Out on the stormy waters. Trying also to hold onto the shore, not willing to let go. This "wind of the spirit" was not a balmy breeze. J suggested that I let go and be out there just for the time I was in the Magic Circle. I said that I was obligated to stay in contact with the shore because I had made the commitment to bring back the fish I caught.

This felt unbelievably difficult. The Fist told me I was getting myself all worked up over nothing. I responded that it certainly didn't feel like "nothing" to me. J agreed and said that this was no place for criticism, that what was happening to me was the tension of trying to hold on to both.

"It feels as though what I'm trying to do is impossible," I cried. "Is it really impossible?"

"It's probably going to feel that way for a while," J replied.

I was holding on to both the conscious (the shore) and the unconscious (the stormy water) while the wind blew and pulled on me. The passion of doing this work added fuel to the tension, because I care so much about it. Even caring about it, however, does not lessen the desire to escape the pain of learning what might be revealed.

I stayed there experiencing this for a long time, until it was time to return to J's office.

There is tension involved in being both inner and outer, high and low, excited and bored, exemplary and blameworthy. It includes both the person I show and the one I hide, the conscious one and its unconscious opposite, the me I know and love and the me I see in all the folks I don't much like. It is me, myself, and I, my own core self, that I am running from when I try to escape, because the tension is so great. Thomas Moore, in *Care of the Soul*, urges one to stretch enough to encompass ones contradictions in order to take care of one's soul. This stretching is none too comfortable.

Becoming more and more who you are sounds so much easier than it is. If you are proud of certain highbrow parts of yourself, making room for the sleaze is not easy. My own husband, lover and main support of my development used to tell me that he loved me just the way I was, "but if you get any more that way, I won't be able to stand you!" When I send the question, "Can you still stand me?" out into the ether, I get the reply, "Thank God I don't have to!"

In my favor, however, is the news that the supply of books to escape into is dwindling. This is no surprise. I have been consuming books in great quantities since before I can remember. How can there be any left? It has always been easier and more pleasant to read than to engage in struggle. I learned it early. Books are wonderful creations and reading is a satisfying experience, but anything used as an escape from what needs to be done takes on an objectionable color. In the weeks that followed these dreams I set myself on a course of staying with the work, and difficult and haphazard as the task was, it brought a response.

Being attacked in a dream can sometimes indicate that your efforts are having an effect against one of your nastier inner characters. The bad guys usually start off overpowering you through trickery or appealing to your usual habits, but when you persist in your efforts to tame them, they often come out in the open and go after you in a graphic and brutal way. Such was the case in this dream:

THE ATTACK

> A man has mutilated my cat, CatScan, torn one of his front legs almost off and crushed his body. He is dying. I can't do anything to save CatScan, so I go after the man with the intention to hurt him badly. But he is much stronger than I am. He picks me up and runs with me through a cavernous brick-walled building, up and down some flights of stairs, toward a wall where he is going to smash me before throwing me off the bluff.

Comments

As soon as I wrote this dream down, I knew that associations and interpretations would not be enough. I had to fight back. So I closed my eyes and re-entered the dream, letting it build in intensity as I shivered with fright. I could not escape from this evil man's grip, but the chattering of my teeth reminded me that I had been brushing and flossing them all these years, waiting for this moment. Disgusting as his flesh was, I sank those teeth into his neck and closed them tightly. I ground them together, and I twisted and pulled and gnawed and ripped.

He was indeed injured. His grip weakened. He sank to the floor, bleeding profusely from the hole in the front of his neck. I extricated myself. I spat out his Adam's apple. He reached out to grab it, but I was too quick. My foot acted instinctively and I ground it with my heel. He tried to howl, but my mouthful of gristle had included his vocal cords, and no sound emerged.

"Now will you leave me alone?" I said coldly, before walking away. I did not intend to stick around and take pity on him.

Several years ago, while working on a dream in which I bit an enemy, I discovered in the *I Ching* Hexagram #21 *Biting Through.* In this hexagram the image is that of an open mouth with an obstruction between the teeth. There is an obstacle in one's life that needs to be bitten through in an energetic way to remove it. Wondering what would happen if I succeeded, I asked that question, then threw another hexagram, which turned out to be #27: *Taking Nourishment.*

This means more than is obvious at a quick glance. In my childhood, my ability to seek nourishment from my mother hinged on taking care of her, protecting her from my father, who threatened to kick her out if anything happened to me. Thus following those rules to placate my father in order to get nourishment from my mother was important. There was an obstacle built in, however, because the rules themselves kept me separated from my core self, my passion, and the source of any real nourishment, any soul food. Therefore, this whole journey involves episodes of *Biting Through.* Gnawing out the enemy's vocal cords is simply one round of a long struggle.

The image of my cat in a dream has several dimensions. CatScan is small and vulnerable and would be easy to destroy because of his trusting nature. But he is also a cat's cat, independent and self sufficient, sucking up to no one for approval. No wonder the forces of evil went after him.

But when I fought back, the evil one attacked me directly. And a few nights later he was back, more dangerous than ever:

VEHICULAR AGGRESSION

> Two vehicles come into the parking area where I am standing. One is a rugged, black, expensive-looking jeep-like vehicle that is being driven aggressively. The other is similar in style, but tan. Both are going fast, and the tan one sideswipes the other very slightly. This enrages the driver of the black vehicle. He turns rapidly and slams his car into the tan one.
>
> Now the tan car pulls back out on the road, trying to escape, but the black one follows fast and rams him from

behind. The tan one speeds up, but the black one catches him easily and slams into him again.

I watch this scene, appalled. The enraged driver seems to have no constraints against doing damage and harm to others and possibly even to himself, although it also seems as though the rage itself protects him and makes his vehicle invulnerable.

Now the angry driver is out of his car. Another onlooker has been using a cell phone to call the police. The angry driver goes after her now. I step in and try to immobilize him by striking at a piece of equipment near the telephone, thinking that it is connected in some way to the enraged man.

But my action only draws his anger toward me. He picks up a hammer and a bullet and bats the bullet at me like a tennis serve. It falls a little short, but then he throws the hammer at me as well. I am frightened, realizing that this man is aggressive, strong, angry and completely oblivious to any fear of consequences. I only hope the other onlooker's call to the police went through and they will arrive before the man kills me.

Comments

It is interesting that there are two vehicles in this dream and I am driving neither. I am standing apart, watching. Could the two vehicles I mentioned, Performance and Maintenance, be at odds with each other? It wouldn't surprise me if this were so, since each is identified with one of my parents, who were not often in agreement with each other.

One moral of these two dreams is that there really is evil in this world we live in. Many religious liberals no longer personify that evil as Satan and picture the demon taking over persons to accomplish evil ends, but that does not mean that the evil itself has vanished. It appears in many forms, large and small, from genocide to the stifling of a single person's spirit. The specific evil, small and personal but tenacious, that attacks me wants my downfall into *abulia*, the condition of being without will power, the complete lack of "cohesive thrust". I have to fight it whenever it comes my way. If I use my various escape techniques such as books, food, Computer Solitaire, etc., the evil wins that round and thereby becomes even stronger.

Taking a stand against evil of whatever form and size is another important spiritual discipline. Often the dreams tell us to act against the evils in society, and when they do, we must respond. It is less obvious that taking a stand against our own small personal evils is important. But if we do not take the responsibility of caring for ourselves, no one else is going to. This small piece of Creation will wither and decay.

It did not dawn on me immediately that the following dream was also about escape. I had to write down some associations to the images before I made the connection.

PRISONERS BUILD A SOD HOUSE

> Off to one side, over to my left and a little behind me, there's a building project going on. At the moment it involves making walls out of sod, fastening strips of sod to hardware cloth, to build the walls of a house. The men doing the work are minimum-security prisoners. I am going over soon to help with the project.

Comments

In this project the building is earthy and humble, grounded, much more down to earth than the buildings going up in the city on the hill. But construction is construction, after all, and not to be sneered at.

The minimum-security prisoners were a mystery to me until I

started writing down various thoughts about prisoners and realized that these were men who could escape but who probably wouldn't. My going to join them, then, might mean subjecting myself to periods of construction labor without allowing myself to escape.

My response to this dream was to delete Solitaire from my computer. The other escapes were not as threatening, because to enact them I would have to leave the computer in my studio and go into the house to read or eat, but Computer Solitaire was right here at hand, tempting me away from constructing my manuscript, and in the process rotting my brain cells and destroying my carpel tunnel. That I was addicted became evident as soon as I went in the house, where I rooted through drawers until I found a deck of cards! I'm now like a whiskey drinker who has switched to beer.

Then I remembered another connection with this sod building. Mmmmm had spoken out many times in distress about having to go on with her performance even when bad things happened to her. In *Daughter of Hearts, Daughter of Clubs* Carrie has to go on with her life even after her father attacks, her brother disappears, and the house falls down.

MMMMM SAYS: Here I am with the house fallen down around me. But I have to ignore the wreckage and pretend that nothing happened. If I don't, even worse things will happen. My mama will have to leave. But while I'm putting on the show that nothing's wrong, I feel myself pour out of my body through my feet. I pour out through my feet under the grass, and I become a little white grub that everybody wants to spray with poison. "Get rid of that worm," everybody says. And I try, but it keeps coming back.

And indeed it did. I remember very few events before I was seven years old, but the following dream is one of them:

THE WORM RETURNS

In the dream I am in my bedroom with the door closed. I hear something at the door. Then whatever it is flattens out and slides under the door through the crack. It's a

> worm riding a tricycle, and it fills out again once it gets in my room.

Comments

As I struggled to accept Mmmmm's presence in my psyche, many hours a week were spent in dialogues, artworks, Magic Circle visits and the construction of four large sketchbooks containing her story in her own words and drawings.

She phrased it in different images at different times, but every version tells the story of the split between the gifted little red-haired girl and the sick, wretched one in hiding. One version is this:

MMMMM SAYS: I was thrown into a dungeon and the door clanged shut and it was never mentioned again, ever, and that's the truth, and people had to tippy-toe forever after, and then I was a good girl. And the other girl was a worm that lived under the house.

SHE SAYS: Good Mmmmm sat with her back against the dungeon door so that Bad Mmmmm couldn't get out.

And now the minimum-security prisoners are building a sod house, a place above ground as a halfway house for the little grub.

As I was working on this section, I had this dream:

EATING THE WORM

> —Now it's time to eat. The food is supposed to be a great delicacy with a chocolate flavor. To my horror it's alive, a bristly chocolate wooly-worm that tries to escape off the plate and across my lap. I grab for it a couple of times, then manage to catch and eat it. It does indeed taste like chocolate. I crunch it right away to give it a quick, easy death and hope that I only have to eat one.

Edinger, in *Anatomy of the Psyche*, explains that eating something incorporates it. The conscious self is able to take in something that has previously been unconscious. He suggests that one always eat whatever food is offered in a dream, even if it is unappealing.

The process goes on. I have no doubt that writing this book contributes to the process even as it describes it. Here, for the first time, I am seeking soul food by biting through the obstacle I always before tried to work around in this old pattern:

abandoned myself

to placate my father

to keep my mother

whose questionable nurture was contingent on my

precocious performance.

Imagine the amount of energy this has taken!

Remember too that I am only one of the persons on this earth. And my circumstances are among the more fortunate. If I, with all the plusses I've had in life, have expended so much energy with so little reward, what of the human condition as a whole?

The situation improves, for me anyway, with the following dream:

THE BANK ROBBERS' ANTIQUE GETAWAY CAR

An antique red car has stopped in the street outside a dentist's office. It is the getaway car of bank robbers. Instead of metal doors and fenders the car has upper and lower side curtains made of heavy red leather gathered on rods like cafe curtains. The passenger, a man, hurries into the dentist's office while the man driving keeps the car in the street with the motor running. After admiring the car, I follow the man into the dentist's office.

Associations

ANTIQUE RED CAR: When my father was young, he went west to work in Colorado making custom auto bodies on Rolls Royce chassis. He loved this work, but he was drafted into the war and never got back to it. Instead he went to work in the automobile plant where his hearing was ruined and his spirit depressed. This red car looks custom built, like a young man's dream car. It's snazzy enough to elevate the image of robbery from something reprehensible to something daring and romantic.

BANK ROBBERS: Money has been stolen from a bank and is now in the car. These robbers are riding around in the most conspicuous getaway car imaginable. This might indicate that psychic energy, represented as money, is being withdrawn from the old Tight Fist father's control (the bank) and placed in the vehicle of the young man's heart's desire.

DENTIST: Very funny! Imagine the bank robber having to stop in mid-getaway to see his dentist! The only connection I could make was the one again of *Biting Through*, of needing to care for my teeth in order to bite through the obstacle to my own nourishment.

The *I Ching's* commentary on Hexagram #21 calls for strength of character and recommends overcoming obstacles that dictate undesirable behavior by being firm and unemotional, yet gentle.

Would that it were so easy to have strength of character!

Comments

J suggested that I live up to this dream by deliberately breaking my father's rules. Doing so was a step into the phase of my life that has become deeply rewarding.

It started by parting with money, an act my father hated. I contributed a substantial amount to help begin the construction of a church building to house the growing Unitarian-Universalist Fellowship I belong to. I did not know at the time what an important step this was in my own process, what it would lead to. I simply had a strong impulse to do it, and I followed that impulse, thumbing my nose at my stingy streak that is personified by my father in dreams.

To help with the construction of a sacred place is like adding to the City on the Hill. The work was done by members of the congregation, in thousands of volunteer hours, and the resulting building is a true church home. It was perhaps the most important event in the congregation's history; it is certainly one of the most important in my own history.

In the last dream of this series the two-car image appears again.

A DISPLAY OF ABANDONED VEHICLES

> I'm at a university where my old writing teacher is giving a reading and workshop. I want to talk with him, but he's surrounded by admirers and I don't want to compete for his attention, so I go close enough for him to see that I'm here and then leave. If he wants to talk to me, he can seek me out.
>
> Now I'm in a large and very odd classroom with display cases like dioramas all around the room. I walk around looking at them. In one is an abandoned vehicle left in a low spot in the ground as landfill. In another the abandoned vehicle has been pushed off a bridge and left as fish habitat. Each one has a plaque that describes in approving terms how much good these junked cars are doing in the present situation.
>
> Now my teacher is here. We talk. After a moment I say, "But what really intrigues me are these two abandoned cars!"

Associations

WRITING TEACHER: Although this teacher has been a fairly frequent inner writer dream figure, I have not seen or corresponded with the actual person for years. I read his books, however, and I notice that he continues writing as he pleases in spite of criticism from his reviewers and suggestions from his editor. Thus his work becomes more and more idiosyncratic the longer he writes. You could not mistake a novel by this man for a work by anyone else.

I believe this authenticity is the quality the Dream Maker is urging on me. Soul work is developmental, and developing means becoming more and more yourself and no one else.

ABANDONED VEHICLES: Here they are, both of them, one being used as land fill, the other as fish habitat. For golden koi, no doubt.

By this point in my journey, I should have discovered some bits of wealth that might help me along my way, and indeed I have.

When I wrote the fantasy, *The Other Real World*, I was not writing what I believed; I was writing what I imagined. But experience has led me into a cautious belief that what I imagined actually happens: when you go into an imagined world, it becomes real; if you don't go, it ceases to exist.

As I gather images, notice them, tend them, inquire into their meaning, it seems as though word gets out and other images start to draw around, interested. They present themselves and invite my attention. I don't have to do it all.

All I have to do is go into a field of images and pay attention. The field then becomes a magnet for *more* images. I get help from beyond myself.

Because I'm not used to it, it's awkward working this way, but I intend to see what happens when I try it more consciously in the next section.

CHAPTER 10

The Field

Sometimes my field of images has appeared as a woods, as in *The Other Real World*, and sometimes as a field of flowers, like a mountain meadow in the summertime, with paintbrush, lupine, and other blossoms scattered everywhere.

WILDFLOWER FIELD

> I'm at a Writers' Conference that's taking place in a big old faded frame house painted pink and white with gray trim like an old-fashioned pastel grandmother. I sink down in a field outside the house. The field is filled with wildflowers.

Comments

As in a number of other dreams, my place is in a field outside but close to the framework of the community of writers, the grandmother that nurtured me with instructions and rewards. In this dream the image is enlarged: it's not just a field, it's a field filled with wildflowers.

But the flower image actually came up earlier, when I was working hard with Mmmmm and her issues. I had the following dream:

THE NOSEGAY

A little girl is making a nosegay of small flowers, different kinds, like the little bouquets given out at the Candlelight Vigil. She selects each flower and places it carefully. "This is the way for you to make the book," she tells me. She's having fun, and I realize that my book can be fun too.

Now there's some kind of trouble involving the police. Maybe she has stolen something. I brace myself.

Associations

CANDLELIGHT VIGIL: This was an annual event sponsored by sexual assault victim assistance programs all over the country, with each community planning its own public recognition of the long-term suffering brought about by sexual assault and/or by the seduction of children. While affiliated with the program in my own community, I participated in several of these vigils. At one of them a survivor of incest who had benefited from our services made little nosegays to give everyone who came.

I myself had been a client who benefited from the local program before becoming an advocate, group facilitator, and a Board member. The quality of service was so good that word got around and women came from miles away, even from larger cities with their own sexual assault programs, to participate. Therapists came to learn from us. To be a part of something so excellent was very rewarding to me.

The little girl in this dream seems to be the flower-picking, fun-loving part of me who was injured by the assaults upon her femininity, Mmmmm, if you will.

BOOK: This book is being created the way the little girl makes her nosegay, with the images themselves working toward their own arrangement.

Another example of the same process is what I often do, walking on one of the beaches here, when I make a pebble arrangement in my open palm, starting with a stone that catches my eye and says, "Choose me!" I then lay it in my hand and continue walking, glancing at it, then glancing down at the beach. When the stone in my hand chooses the next stone, I pick it up, and the next and the next. Sometimes the arrangement progresses smoothly; other times I drop some or all of the pebbles and start over. But the process is always the same: that first stone chooses the next and the next until my palm has the day's arrangement laid out upon it in whatever aesthetic harmony has come about.

Soon after having this dream I came to my studio with my mind a blank page. I sat down and wrote at the top of a page, "The Rules." Then my pencil was taken over by some autonomous force within and I wrote this:

HOW TO MAKE A NOSEGAY

Have a lot of flowers, she says
Have some leaves too, and ferns and vines.
They cover the damp ground. So many,
    piled like pebbles at the shoreline.
Their odor climbs the chilly air -
Carnations in a cooler.

The baby's *breath* is where you start,
    a spray of milky inspiration
    to frame the whole bouquet.
Now turn your mind around and make it look
    the other way
While hand and eye choose a fat bud,
A beginning, like the first word,
    the word that shapes the breath.
The rest is easy.

A story line will spin itself
While that first bud chooses the next
    and the next
Until your hand is full, and the last
    sprig says, The End!
Then tie the vine around the stems
And toss the nosegay to the wind.

Later that day I had an appointment scheduled with J, but I had a hard time getting there because of confusion about the time or maybe the day, a lot of confusion. I didn't want to go, in spite of feeling that I needed to. I talked out loud to myself on the way over and I prayed for insight.

Beside yourself is how you feel when you're totally distraught, not yourself at all. I was not "beside myself." I was *alongside myself*. I felt doubled. I was Marcia, the person I'm used to, who manages daily life and gets along just fine, or at least okay, and someone else alongside who needed a voice, some attention. It was a very strange sensation, but strange sensations are not at all uncommon when you're doing this work.

"What do you need?" J asked as soon as I told him how I was feeling. I needed some Magic Circle time.

And there she was, the little girl from my dream, thin and white and freckled, hair bright as a flame. I could see her as a photo of myself, wearing my brown sun suit with the big white spots, squinting in the sunshine.

Then she was in a concrete crypt-like room, like the old bunkers at the nearby fort, where I often walk. There was a telephone in the imagined bunker, and she wanted to call for help, to dial 911, but if she took the receiver down, the bad noise would come and get her, the noise that comes if you leave the phone off the hook.

Then the phone rang. What a shock!

I got derailed here, because the image that intruded was insistent, but it didn't fit what I thought was going on. "There's a censorship problem here," I was finally able to say. "This doesn't fit."

J replied, "Something doesn't fit with what's already there. Go ahead and say it."

"Well," my Mmmmm voice answered, "it's Malcolm." It was Malcolm X again, the revolutionary who had appeared in my imagination before in a different context. "Malcolm X, who calls me up when I'm in the bunker. It's something about the revolution."

"Ask him what he wants," J suggested.

"Well, it's something about hope. He says he calls people up in the bunkers to tell them there's hope." Here I began sobbing out loud, hard. "I can't stand that," said my Mmmmm voice. "I can't stand any of it. I can't stand to have hope."

"It's hard to hope for something," said J.

"Yes. When you have hope, you put your hand up out of the bunker for help, and they come along and mow your fingers off." I cried and cried. "I don't have hope," cried my Mmmmm voice. "What I do is a little dance. I see something that I might hope for, if I could have hope. And then I put myself in the way of it, even though I can't hope for it."

"What would you hope for?" asked J.

"Just to do the flowers," said wistful Mmmmm. "Just to do the flowers."

"Maybe Malcolm can help you," J suggested. "How might he help?"

Then the scene changed. I was outside the bunker, in a meadow of flowers. "It would have to be a moveable Magic Circle where I was safe. It would have rolls of razor wire around it, and Malcolm would be there on the outside as a guard. He would have on that thing," and here I had to struggle for the word, "that thing," and I gestured, "a bandolier."

"With ammunition," said J.

"Grenades like medjool dates. An assault weapon. A machine gun. A rifle." I gestured again, two hands making a long rifle. "And I am safe in there and can just do the flowers." She meant that she could make the nosegay. "He can keep all the lawn order from getting me."

(Remember here the rule that says to be sure you keep the grass mowed before you indulge in flowers. That's the lawn order.)

I stayed in the meadow for a while and enjoyed it, but soon anxiety washed over me again. Something was going to go wrong. This couldn't last.

Then my father got an airplane and flew over dropping leaflets.

"You're getting a lot of propaganda," said J.

"The police are here," cried my Mmmmm voice. "I can't stay with the flowers."

"How would Malcolm deal with the police?" J asked.

"He would sit in a tree like Sgt. York and pick them off one by one." Mmmmm thought about this for a moment.

Then intense longing washed over me, the longing to be able to work on my book the way the little girl makes the nosegay. And it was time to come back to the ordinary world. I went home and wrote down in my journal what had happened.

It has taken a long time and a lot of this kind of imaginal work for this longing to be fulfilled. The forces of "lawn order" did not go down willingly. Nor do they stay away permanently. The drawing on the next page is entitled "Wildflowers Encroaching Lawn Order Encroaching". Lawn Order is the stronger, still.

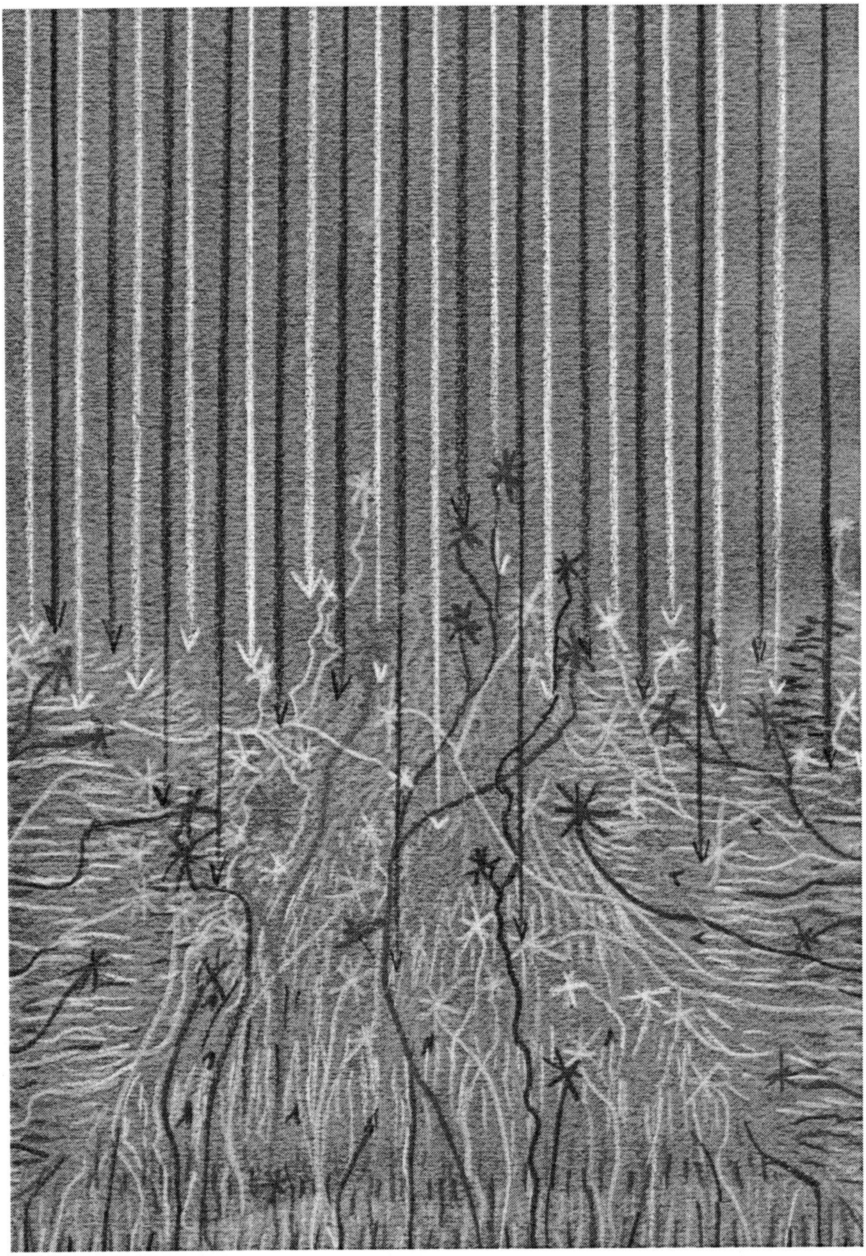

Wildflowers Encroaching Lawn Order Encroaching

PART 3

Going Down

CHAPTER 11

The Neighborhood

The question arises: Why do it this way? Why follow *this* path, accept *this* discipline? Why spend time and effort on a soul journey in the first place, and once embarked, why not follow one of the already-mapped spiritual paths of the world's religions instead of flopping around in the thorn bushes of my own dreams? And why choose *these* dreams instead of a different set? There are hundreds to choose from. Another selection might tell a different story, a better story.

How do I know I'm getting it right?

Doubts about the value of what I'm doing and my ability to do it paralyze me. Every newspaper or magazine I pick up during such a period has a learned article by some expert, about dreams being *nothing but* random squirts of some polysyllabic chemical in the brain. The deity, too, is a Nothing Butta. *Quote of the Day* on my computer throws out this from H. L. Mencken: "God is the immemorial refuge of the incompetent, the helpless, the miserable. They find not only sanctuary in His arms, but also a kind of superiority, soothing to their macerated egos: He will set them above their betters." [6]

Thus, even if my Ego is sufficiently macerated (softened up by soaking—presumably in the brine of my miserable tears) for me to find God,

6. From *Minority Report: H. L. Mencken's Notebooks*

I'll still have Mencken to deal with, not to mention my betters, to whom I pledge that if God does set me above them, they needn't worry: I won't tell.

I used to read my work-in-progress aloud at the open mike bar where Writers' Center people gathered. If anyone left to go pee, I would cut that part out of the story. If the manuscript won the War of the Bladders, I knew it was okay. But now, without the open mike, without collective review and critique, without any collective interest in the matter except to scorn it, how do I know I'm getting it right?

In answer comes a dream:

GETTING IT RIGHT

> I am walking in my childhood neighborhood, heading away from the house toward downtown. The street is like an obstacle course. Bushy hedges have to be struggled through; thickets with branches at face level make it impossible to see where I'm going.
>
> Measuring my progress is done with a board that has pegs stuck into it. I have to weave strands of thread between the pegs, and it has to come out right, with all the ends long enough to tie but not so long that they dangle. The threads are blue, and there are a lot of them, and all the pegs and all the strands make an endless number of possible ways to do the lacing. I get the threads woven through the pegs so that there is a bunch of ends, a handful, just long enough to tie in a single knot but not a double. I know they will come untied again, but I go on anyway.

Associations

THE NEIGHBORHOOD: The neighborhood of childhood is what some of us try to escape, the reason why boys in the ghetto learn to box and play basketball. It's the place we picked up information about who we were supposed to be and what our possibilities were. Being back in the neighborhood in a dream tells me that I still have business there. I am still questioning who I am and what my possibilities are.

DOWNTOWN: If a city represents one's central core, even more so does the downtown. In THE RED CAR AND THE CITY ON THE HILL the city being built high on the hill was an image of the *realized* center, while one's hometown in a dream is an image of the *given* center. We are born with the latter through grace, but we develop the city on the hill through our own efforts, assisted by grace.

THE BUSHY HEDGES: The word "hedge" has another meaning besides "bushes" or "barrier." A "hedge" is a means of protection or defense against loss, something that reduces risk, especially the risk of inflation. When you hedge your bets, you bet on both horses or buy both stocks, committing yourself to neither.

That's like seesawing between needing collective approval for what I'm doing and taking a dream like this as a valuable message from within. My lack of faith in my own path, the fact that I hedge my bets by looking outward for assurance of its value, this hedging makes it harder to get to the center of town.

A "hedge" is also an intentionally unclear or indirect statement.

As a person who sustained some losses while a child in the neighborhood, I find myself hedging more often than I like. The hedge is like Carrie's wrap of razor wire. It's like the lengths I go to not to feel inflated for fear of being brought down. It's using the word "seems" a lot in order to avoid the word "is."

I believe, also, that it means having to *borrow* inspiration, borrow faith and trust because I am too much afraid of inflation to find my own.

I borrow faith and trust and inspiration by projecting these qualities on someone else who then becomes necessary to my progress. My therapist, J, was one such person. He's the one who was able to make the Magic Circle and invite the spirits. Earlier in this book Mmmmm admitted that it was J's faith in the spirits, not her own, that brought forth her ability to trust. Borrowing these qualities by associating with someone else who has them is easier than looking for them in myself. It requires less investment.

THREADS: Weaving the threads first one way and then another to make progress reminds me once again that constructing this manuscript is *part* of my soul journey, not just an *account* of it. Weaving is a good metaphor for what I'm doing here, testing this dream and that, keeping one, deleting others, fastening them together with commentary and associations, trying not to say the same thing as many times in the manuscript as I've had to learn it over and over again in waking life, trying not to leave too many dangling ends.

COMMENTS: The same people, *and I am one of them*, who mouth the platitude that there isn't any single right way are the very ones who then worry themselves to death trying to find it. It takes a dream like this to remind me that there *really* isn't any single right way. We lace the threads, gather the images, tie up the package with nothing dangling — and then it all comes loose again and the process starts over, like making nosegays and pebble arrangements, like life itself.

The question of choice, why choose this instead of that, is possible only in a culture that is based on an assumption of so much free will that any kind of deterministic speculation is scorned as a way of avoiding responsibility for one's own situation, of blaming destiny for one's failures.

I believe that my choices are only partially free. Sometimes when I'm squalling because my husband is dead and my knee hurts and my car sounds funny, I feel a tug and realize that I am being reeled in, whistled home. Sometimes I really do feel that I'm doing what I'm doing because it is my destiny to take this path and that the losses I sustained in the neighborhood were part of that destiny.

I also believe that the requirement is not only to choose the path to your true self from moment to moment, as opportunities arise and as best you can, but also to accept the discipline, the rigors and the rewards of the path you're on. Gazing off toward someone else's path wastes a lot of time.

The path I am on originated back in the neighborhood of childhood in a dream I will add later. When my present movement and progress get difficult or painful, then going back to the neighborhood for information helps things along.

The following poem celebrates the possibility of leaving the old neighborhood for one in another dream in which I was able to bound and soar instead of pushing my way through the hedges:

TO LEAVE THE NEIGHBORHOOD

Hedges hamper her in the cramped
and brambly place she calls home.
To move requires she wield a brave machete
and risk some bloody scratches if she oversteps.
To stay is to be overgrown.

No wonder this new neighborhood
attracts her so, its lights and peopled streets
under arching beeches so old their roots
heave the pavement. With the wind
at her back, her steps soar.

But there is work to do at home
before she walks away: a final clearing,
a barn to take apart for the old wood.
The animals too have outgrown
what they've always known is true.

But not yet. A few days after the triumph of finishing a long section of this book, I must have been feeling too good about my success. Perhaps I forgot to hedge myself against inflation. There were the images, how fascinating! There was my emerging belief that if I went there, the images would come. But not long after I finished the manuscript, a miasma of doubt began to pollute the air and choke off my breathing. Only days earlier I had written these happy lines in my journal: "My lungs have new rooms filled with fresh air. I am stalked by smiles."

But now my Cold Fishy Eye got the upper hand. I began to doubt the whole process, doubt what I had said about the images, began to suspect that I'd gotten too big for my britches, had claimed too much territory for my own. What did I mean by announcing that if I go there, the images will show up? Had I forgotten my old sense of myself as a wallflower? Who am I, after all, to attract the images' interest and become a vehicle for their expression? Why would they choose me?

And believing that I was such an unattractive vehicle, how could I trust them not to stand me up? There was really something wrong now. The images were there, and I was here, and I had established a conduit in between, but my lack of trust was like a broken place in the conduit. If I felt like a wallflower even to the images, how could I bear to come to the dance at all, expecting to sit humiliated and forlorn on the sidelines?

CHAPTER 12

In Wallflower Territory

THE WALLFLOWER WOMAN'S HOME

While going to school I am staying at the home of the Wallflower Woman. She doesn't like her husband and is planning to leave him. I tell her that he's not so bad and that she's lucky to have him.

She creates more and more of a mess the longer I'm here. If a chair has two things on it one minute, it will have six things on it the next time I look.

I can't get my own things together for school because of the mess. One day I go to band practice and realize that I've forgotten my clarinet.

Back at the house, the Wallflower Woman has washed all my clothes, and there they are in a wrinkled heap that now I'll have to iron.

I go to the basement to get something. The stairs are very narrow, only a foot across and open on one side to the floor below. The Wallflower Woman has made them even more hazardous by putting up racks on the wall where a handrail would be more helpful.

Now I'm ironing my clothes. There is no room for anything, no room to put a garment after it's ironed, no room, even on the ironing board itself. Things stick to each other and stick to my fingers and stick to the iron. "I can't work under these conditions," I say.

But I continue to try. I start to iron a pair of brown slacks. There are bulges in the pockets. I pull out a wadded up handkerchief, a tan leather work glove and a book of quotations, all of which went through the washer and dryer. "I just can't work under these conditions," I repeat.

Associations

WALLFLOWER WOMAN'S HOME: The Wallflower Woman is a dream character who can resemble any one of several women I have known, each of whom has been the kind of unattractive girl who never gets asked out on a date, who can find a husband only by mail order or signing on as a nursemaid to his motherless children or aged parents. She's the kind who has never received a Valentine, not even in first grade when they came forty to a package and there were only thirty kids in the class. She is how I sometimes feel about myself.

Often the setting of a dream marks off the kind of psychic territory the dreamer is in, even in waking life. This dream says, "It's as if you were within the aura of this woman, under her influence. She's the boss here."

Why Wallflower Woman doesn't like her husband is not spelled out, but I remind her how lucky she is to have a husband at all. She'd better stay with someone she doesn't like because that's all she can get. The fact that I advise her this way indicates that my Ego (who is the "I" in a dream) comes down on this side of the struggle, which is what makes it so hard to pull myself out of this sticky complex. It's as though I'm telling myself, "Yes, you really are so repulsive no one would want you. You really will be rejected if you go for what you want." With my Ego inside the complex, helping it along, there's nowhere to get any traction to pull myself out of it. This is one house I ought to back out from quickly! But I'm not able. Oh House Cleaner, where are you, now that I need you?

And how does this wallflower business translate into my present situation? I am a widow with an intense and rewarding love behind me. Another lover is not what I find myself thinking about or hoping for; in fact, Vance would be one tough act to follow. It's my connection with the images and the creative spirit that absorbs me now.

But the fact that I urge the Wallflower Woman further into wallflowerism is not a good sign, not a good sign at all. A woman in this situation is terribly vulnerable to exploitation by opportunistic men, because she has no faith in her ability to attract the one she chooses. Within her aura I have no faith I can attract the images, and I become vulnerable to picking up on all the free-floating sneers that are out there, the sneers about dream work, soul work, personal work, the messages that the marketplace is the only determiner of value, that the inner determiner is a Nothing Butta.

In the dream this Wallflower Woman is someone who creates such a mess that I can't possibly work. She attends to my garments in a way that makes them unwearable. Her supposed favor in doing my laundry was not a favor at all but an invasion *disguised* as a favor. There's something of the spirit contained in my dresses and blouses and shoes and skirts, as later dreams will demonstrate. For them to go through this woman's wash is disastrous.

WALLFLOWER WOMAN'S BASEMENT: Getting into the basement is difficult. I cannot readily make contact with the deeper realm, which is where the images live. Contrast the Wallflower Woman's basement with one in another, happier dream:

CONNECTING BASEMENTS

> In a large old house I go to the basement, which has walls of crumbling brick. There are several rooms and a number of cupboards. One cupboard door falls to pieces as I open it. I realize with pleasure that I can replace the door

> or not, as I please, because the house belongs to me.
>
> Now I see that there are outer doors and windows in these rooms, facing onto dark streets, that my basement is connected with the whole town's basement, like in the Seattle Underground.

Such a basement implies that when I'm centered in my own house, I have a connection to the larger community by virtue of my "underground" work of bringing unconscious material into consciousness and inviting others to do the same. But in the basement of the Wallflower Woman, I can't even get down the stairs safely. I quit believing in what I do.

SCHOOL: I'm in a state of learning. The particular school indicated by this dream is teaching me to recognize the conditions that make me unable to work.

BAND PRACTICE: I was once a music student, and for one semester I had to take a course in how to play the clarinet. It was during that semester that I got sick. The sickness gave me the excuse I needed to convince my father that I should drop out of music school. Thus I associate playing clarinet with reverting to sickness and making important choices in an unhealthy way, not going toward something I actually want, but fleeing in disarray from something I'm *supposed to want and even want to want*, but don't really.

The Wallflower Woman, of course, can't make choices toward anything she wants. She doesn't even *know* what she wants, because she's convinced that it won't do her any good to know. How unpleasant it is to be faced with this image in the mirror and to know whose reflection it is!

STICKY THINGS: Everything in this horrible environment is sticky. It reminds me of how, when one has a belief rooted in forgotten and thus unexamined experience, other messages stick to it, like the things I read in the paper about Nothing Butta. My waking life experience as a lover did not bear up the belief that I was a repulsive wallflower woman, but

I continued to believe it anyway, bolstered by random words in books, movies, and TV. No wonder I began to feel that the images themselves would recognize my inherent wallflowerishness and reject me! "I can't work under these conditions!" When I am in the house of the Wallflower Woman, I cannot possibly make contact with the images.

And I couldn't. I didn't. I sat on the block and watched the work pile up.

GOING THROUGH THE WASH: A handkerchief, of course, can go through the wash just fine, except for the loss of the brine of tears to macerate my Ego. But a leather work glove will suffer and a book of quotations even more. My work gloves are big and tough and used to handle the wood for my stove. And I know exactly what happens when a book goes through the wash: it happened to my bird book; Peterson's pages stuck together, with my Life List in between.

Going through the wash is, in the most mundane terms possible, a process that Edinger describes in *Anatomy of the Psyche* as akin to baptism, an immersion in something greater than the ego, which cleanses and revives ones hopes — the *solutio* of alchemy. The *solutio* dissolves or melts beliefs that have become hardened, and then a "solution" to the problem may more easily be found. My beliefs about my wallflower self need such dissolving. But for me to notice the problem, the Dream Maker supplied me with a dream that put my belongings into a polluting immersion in the Wallflower Woman's Maytag.

A little later in his book Edinger writes about the dissolving of a body of old belief being necessary for the next step: the embodiment of the Spirit must move to where you can really feel it. You know it's there when you feel *inspired*.

Comments

There's a hint about Spirit in GETTING IT RIGHT where there are hedges I have to struggle through. Those hedges protect me from the risk of inflation, which is the danger inherent in the presence of Spirit. Inspiration is by nature inflating, and for a person trained from infancy to avoid having anything happen to her, the safe bet is to risk nothing, to prick balloons and take the wind out of sails before anything happens. I'd best not hope for too much, claim too much territory.

C. G. Jung talked about the Spirit in an interesting (and readable) lecture. Here are a few of his remarks:

> In keeping with its original wind-nature, spirit is always an active, winged, swift-moving being as well as that which vivifies, stimulates, incites, fires, and inspires. To put it in modern language, spirit is the dynamic principle, forming for that very reason the classical antithesis of matter — the antithesis, that is, of its stasis and inertia. Basically it is the contrast between life and death. [7]

The birds mentioned earlier represent spirit.

And, "The hallmarks of spirit are, firstly, the principle of spontaneous movement and activity; secondly, the spontaneous capacity to produce images independently of sense perception; and thirdly, the autonomous and sovereign manipulation of these images." [8]

The autonomy of these images is the sense that they come to me, rather than that I make them happen.

My dreary wallflower problem began with a little girl who lost her spirit in the underbrush of the neighborhood. This dream came on a Valentine's Day:

THE GIRL IN THE SAILOR DRESS

> The dream involves a little girl of seven or so wearing a dark blue sailor dress. Something has happened to her that took away her spirit.

7. C. J. Jung, *Collected Works*, Volume Nine, Part One
8. Ibid.

Associations

THE GIRL IN THE SAILOR DRESS: In the family photo box is a picture of me taken in late October before I turned seven in January. I am wearing a sailor dress. Several photos were taken that day. With me in one of them is my half-brother just before he turned eighteen; I am holding a jack-o-lantern. In another photo he is looking pious, holding a Bible. In this one I look sick, as if I might throw up. Maybe I did, I don't remember.

Something happened around that time that caused my brother to leave our home for good without finishing high school, thus abandoning his hope of becoming a doctor. His room, which he had converted into a laboratory, became the guest room, all the test tubes and flasks and burners now gone. I don't know what happened: the event of his leaving and most of my life before then is beyond the power of my memory. But the aftermath included my long illness with a stay in the hospital. It included my father's rage and his suspicious eye always gazing in my direction. It included my turning away from and distrusting God. And finally, over the years, the aftermath included my brother's never missing an opportunity to assure me that my body was gross and distasteful to him. In the present I am reminded of this era of my childhood when I find my spirit gone and my body dragging itself around through a heavy world.

I felt more than one way about my brother's disappearance. On the one hand, the laboratory of his room was a scary place. Mmmmm made a picture (see next page) about which she said: "My heart is like a specimen frog that wishes it could hop away whenever someone comes close with sharp tools." She often remarked that she hated being somebody's experiment.

On the other hand, she felt abandoned when he left:

MMMMM SAYS: He's gone. I am nobody's Valentine now, just a wallflower, and I can't even cry about it, can't even mention that I miss him or I'll make my father even madder than he already is. "What the hell's the matter with you?" my father yells at me if he catches me looking sad.

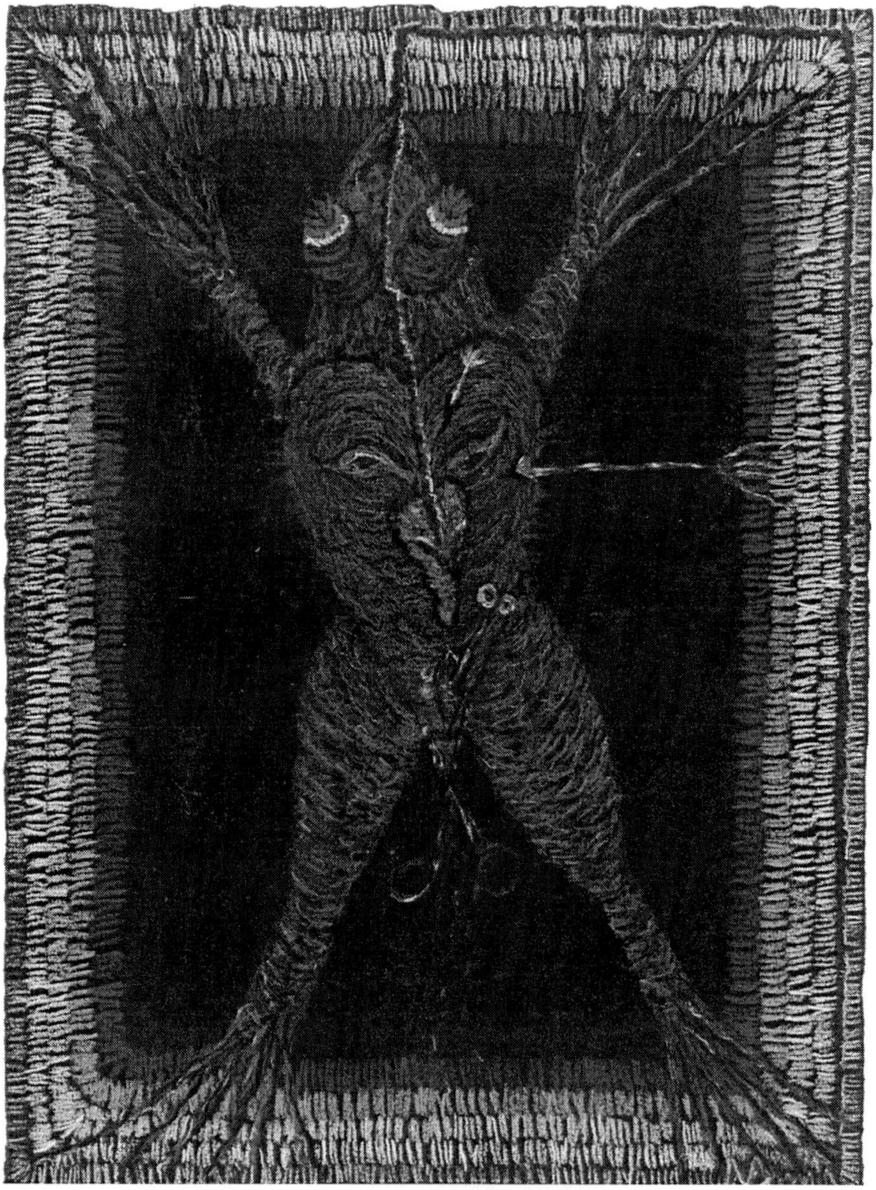

Specimen Frog

I don't know the answer, but there must be something the matter with me, or I wouldn't be a wallflower, would I? I would still be his Valentine. He would still say, "Sis is my girl, aren't you, Sis?"

I was just that age, still in first grade, when I had this dream, which I consider an early "orientation" dream:

COMMUNICATION

> Someone teaches me the word "communication." I learn it easily.

The next day at school during "Show and Tell" I told the dream and printed the word on the blackboard. My best friend from childhood reminds me of this event every so often.

A wiser teacher might have taken me aside and asked me kindly what I needed to communicate. But rarely is anyone that wise. My teacher instead praised me for knowing what such a big word meant and being able to spell and print it so well.

"Taking your mind off it" only represses it to torment you later. "Putting it behind you" has the same effect, with the added concern about constantly watching your backside lest you be nipped in the behind at any moment. "Snapping out of it" is even worse, because it uses every bit of energy you have to do the snapping.

My mother tried to help me take my mind off my brother's disappearance, while my father's warning was that I'd better snap out of it, and quickly.

I understood. Expressing my grief and bewilderment was forbidden. It would mean that *something had happened to me*, and I remembered well my father's threat to kick my mother out if this occurred. My silence would protect my mother. No wonder I dreamed of communication.

I lost my freedom of expression. My efforts to regain it have helped to shape my life, for better or worse. Finding my own voice, hearing my own music, attaining the freedom of speech that is supposed to be guaranteed to all U. S. citizens: these tasks have taken many years.

LOSS OF SPIRIT: The loss of expressive freedom was not the only thing that happened. The dream says that the little girl in the sailor dress lost her spirit. And Mmmmm says she lost her Valentine and became a wallflower. When my brother left home so precipitously and under such dark circumstances, he carried a lot of my spirit away with him.

The following is the first dream I recorded when I began keeping a journal years later.

NO MORE DANCING

> I am in a laboratory. A stylized female pelvis is on a table being worked on. One of the men there suggests that they all go ahead and rape the pelvis, which is a virgin. Another replies that it's too ugly and undesirable to rape. I then stab the pelvis with a fork.
>
> Now I am with a group of young women dressing to dance, pulling on our leotards, lacing up our shoes. The others all go out and dance, but I can't. Instead I hide in the closet and cry.

Losing the ability to dance is the same as losing spirit. Being unable to dance occurs in the second scene of this dream, and the dream's structure seems to be *if this, then that.* The implication is that what happens here is an outgrowth of what happened in the first scene. I wonder whether I'd have danced then if, in the first scene, instead of stabbing the female pelvis, I had stabbed the men to punish them for their disrespect. But instead, I joined them in their scorn.

There is something of my brother present in this laboratory setting. It was my brother's room that was furnished as a lab, with a folding cot for him to sleep on.

By his continual assertion that his sister's body repelled him, my brother helped me to choose the lesser of evils in a no-win situation. If he found me attractive, then something might have happened to bring down my father's wrath, which could cause me to lose my mother. If not, then I was repulsive, and no wonder my brother left. Not an easy choice to make, and not one made consciously. I chose to keep my mother and accept myself as repulsive.

Since that time, feminists have challenged the pervasive disrespect that many women absorb into their very bodies, which they then torment in their efforts to become more desirable (and thus more worthy of rape). I was late in discovering feminism or I might have learned earlier to fight instead of absorb, and I would not be having dreams about loss of spirit this late in life.

The next dream addresses the issue in a slightly different way:

FINDING MY OWN MUSIC

> Scene 1: A nursing home official says something condescending to me phrased in a way that avoids the responsibility for insult. I respond to the insult, including the insult of couching it that way, speaking to him sharply and to the point. I'm afraid people will dislike me for this, but then I find out that I have given voice to what they too were feeling.
>
> Scene 2: I'm with a chorus, standing behind all the others. A song begins. I sing along, but the woman in front of me turns to me impatiently, and I realize that I'm singing in a different key.
>
> Scene 3: I am looking out an upstairs window when a young man comes up behind me and holds me there by wrapping his arms around me. He's blond, with a Greek profile, and he's flushed and panting as though he's been

running a long way. His body is warm and feels good close to me.

Now he maneuvers me outdoors with his arms still tight around me. The chorus is gathering on a big verandah. He pulls me away from them onto the grounds of this establishment, which looks like the VCCA (Virginia Center for the Creative Arts) grounds with rolling hills, blue mountains and boxwood hedges. I am getting frightened. I struggle to get free of the man's grasp, but he won't let go. Finally I scream for help. Another man appears, whereupon the young man holding me lets go and runs away.

Now I'm back with the chorus. A poet friend of mine is here. Off to one side is a wire where some birds are hung with clothespins. "Do you see those birds?" I ask my friend. "I think they're lyrebirds." Then I notice that they're dressed in navy blue clothing like I used to wear as a child. Their tail feathers hang out under the garments.

Associations

NURSING HOME: The first story I wrote as a beginning writer was set in a nursing home, and when I saw what I had written in that story, I realized what would happen to me if I continued in my comfortable, protected niche doing what was expected of me. It was like the time that Destiny told Carrie that she'd better be on her way because she was sliding toward the nursing home.

The story I wrote is about an old woman who is given a star-shaped emerald brooch and dreams of dancing in the light cast by the jewels, but ends up hiding the brooch in a hole in her urine-soaked mattress because it is too late for her to dance.

It was written in response to a bizarre sentence that simply popped into my mind: "Mrs. Linton's birthday came early this year." I wrote the story to discover what a sentence like that could mean, but when it was finished, I realized that I had to change my life — and I did, drastically.

SPEAKING SHARPLY: What I was never allowed to do as a child or learned to do as a young woman. After I began writing, however, I started to incorporate one of the things I admired most about Vance: his ability to speak sharply without being afraid of the consequences. Now that he is dead, the whole task of speaking out belongs to me. This is a significant change for me, from being a mush-mouth to being forthright. Speaking sharply and to the point is like stabbing in dream language, and this time I am stabbing the insulter instead of the insulted.

INSULT WITHOUT RESPONSIBILITY: Some people are masters of this technique. I've been guilty of it myself. Condescension wrapped in solicitude is one of its variations. A sharp message wrapped in humor is another. The only way to stop it in other people is to notice it and respond directly to the insult. The only way to stop it in oneself is to strive for authenticity and practice directness.

GIVING VOICE TO WHAT OTHERS FEEL TOO: Connecting basements. Many times people have responded to what I've written by speaking out about similar feelings and experiences. It's as though I go out on a limb, only to find that I'm not alone on it.

I titled this dream FINDING MY OWN MUSIC because I've been the recipient of another insult without responsibility from my brother, this one connected with music.

My brother played the piano, having taken lessons while I was still a toddler, but I ended up taking lessons longer than he did, many years longer, and by the time I was twenty years old and practicing five or six hours a day, I played quite well. He liked to brag about my playing, and when people complimented him on his own music, he would say, "You ought to hear *Sis* play the piano. She can *really* play." But then in the next breath he would turn around and say, "But Sis thinks she's too good for *our* kind of music, don't you, Sis?"

A musical education does instill some snobbery, but my question here should have been "What is *my* kind of music?" I didn't know enough to ask. I did not realize that all those hours of piano practice were spent on my mother's kind of music, the kind that would give her something to be proud of, her ticket into the middle class. Having a musical child who could play Beethoven and Liszt and Chopin on the piano was proof that she had made it. I couldn't tell the difference between what I wanted for myself and what I wanted to give to my mother, to whom I was devoted. I knew that I felt unhappy, but when you're considered the lucky one of the family, it feels ungrateful to be unhappy, and you try hard to feel some other way instead.

Although my brother probably intended no harm to me, his rejection embedded in praise would leave me immobilized, transfixed, with no place to be myself and ask my own belated questions.

The difficulties this has caused me should not be underestimated. Many sessions with J were spent in the Magic Circle contacting the part of me that hung there immobile.

MMMMM SAYS: There's no *way* to be and no *place* to be and so I have decided *not* to be. I have cancelled myself out. I have no qualities, no description, and no image. When they point the camera, I disappear. When they develop the film, there's a blank spot. I am completely focused on not-being.

J SAYS: Describe the place where you're not-there.

MMMMM SAYS: It's padded and very tight. I am growing, but the space where I'm not-here doesn't grow. There's a lot of pressure all around.

J SAYS: Like a pupa?

MMMMM SNARLS: I know what a pupa is! And I know what happens when the pupa breaks open. The butterfly comes out. And then if you're beautiful, you get collected and that means formaldehyde and a pin stuck through you. If you are plain white, you get sprayed with malathion because they think you'll ruin their cabbages.

A DIFFERENT KEY: The dream, FINDING MY OWN MUSIC, turns completely around here, as though to show me first what happens when I take my own stand and then what happens when I try to follow what others are doing. I sing, but I'm not in the right key. People know this and hush me up. I might as well not sing at all as try to sing the Collective's song.

The "Collective" is the name sometimes given to the swarm of inner voices that invite or urge one to follow the conventional wisdom, to pay attention to what people think, not to get out of line. It's our inner representation of the outer groups we are part of, or hope to be part of. At its best it instills a "decent Respect to the Opinions of Mankind".[9] At its worst it keeps you constantly worrying about being okay. In this dream the Collective is represented by the chorus I keep trying to fit into.

UPSTAIRS WINDOW: Here I have a chance to get some distance and to view the situation from a place of thoughtful consideration. The subsequent events indicate that I did not get the message.

YOUNG MAN: A few more words from the work of Jung quoted above: "....the spirit can also take the form of a boy or a youth. In women he corresponds to the so-called 'positive' animus who indicates the possibility of conscious spiritual effort."[10]

This man approaches me at the upstairs window, a place where conscious spiritual effort might happen. I am, in fact, seized. Seized by the spirit, if you will. At first I do not struggle; his body is warm and I like having him close. He is not an ordinary young man. The Greek profile gives him a look of antiquity, and his flushed and panting state make me think he's a long distance runner. I could surely use such an inner character, one who has the strength, endurance, and cohesive thrust to go the distance.

Then he tries to drag me away from the chorus, the Collective, which here is a specific Collective: that of artistic endeavor and

9. *Declaration of Independence*
10. C. J. Jung *Collected Works* ibid.

accomplishment. VCCA is a wonderful artists' colony that offers residencies for writers, musicians and visual artists whose work is deemed worth support. I spent a month there once and loved it. I not only liked the stimulating atmosphere of art-in-progress, the open studio evenings, the performing of newly-composed music and newly-written poetry, I also liked being in the company of those considered worth support, being part of the writing community that includes the poet friend who appears in this dream. But the young man is trying to drag me away from this milieu.

What's wrong with this community, one might ask. Nothing at all. It's quite wonderful. But if I am engaging in a spiritual discipline, doing soul work, attending to images that want expression, making nosegays, then I need to place myself where that can happen. VCCA's support is for art, not religion.

In my dream, WILDFLOWER FIELD, my place is in a field nearby but separated from this community, a place where I do not lose sight of literary values while doing my own work. I am urged again and again by the Dream Maker to follow my own path, but in FINDING MY OWN MUSIC I resist. Here I try to stay with people I enjoy and admire instead of going off into the boxwood hedges alone with this hot and urgent Spirit boy.

And what is the result?

HUNG UP BIRDS: How interesting that these representations of immobilized Spirit are lyrebirds, so called because their tail feathers fan out in the shape of a lyre, which my dictionary defines as "A stringed instrument of the harp family used to accompany a singer or reader of poetry, especially in ancient Greece." Their lyre-shaped tails associate them with the young man who has a Greek profile, while their clothing associates them with my childhood. They are pinned by their clothing instead of flying free.

The result of my trying to stay with artistic endeavor is being hung up, blocked. Better I should go off into the boxwood hedges with the hot young man.

Comments

Jung's "so-called 'positive' animus" is a concept muddy enough to have attracted a lot of diverse interpretation. But it's safe to say that he is a representation or personification of a woman's unconscious masculine qualities, whatever her own unrecognized masculinity is all about, whatever she is attracted to in men, projects on men, and needs to recognize and/or develop in herself. In my dreams he often appears as a helpful workman, but sometimes he comes on pretty strong, as in this dream, and I get frightened and break the connection.

Some of the homework of my soul journey is to establish connection with him whenever possible, which I do through dialogues, through making pictures and sculptures, and through inviting imaginal characters and writing poems.

I asked him once, "*Who am I to you?*" He spoke right up: "*You are my home.*"

Thus I get acquainted with him: that is, with my own inner masculine self. Getting acquainted, however, is only the first step. Next comes asking myself what he would do under certain difficult circumstances, and then doing it. What this often means is going ahead with something I can't do, don't know how to do, or am afraid to do. Acts involving physical courage come to mind. But now it's psychological courage that is more often called for.

What would it mean to allow the young man to drag me away from such a coveted and cosseting Collective as VCCA?

Perhaps I would spend less time hung up. (See next page for Mmmmm's representation of how being hung up looks.)

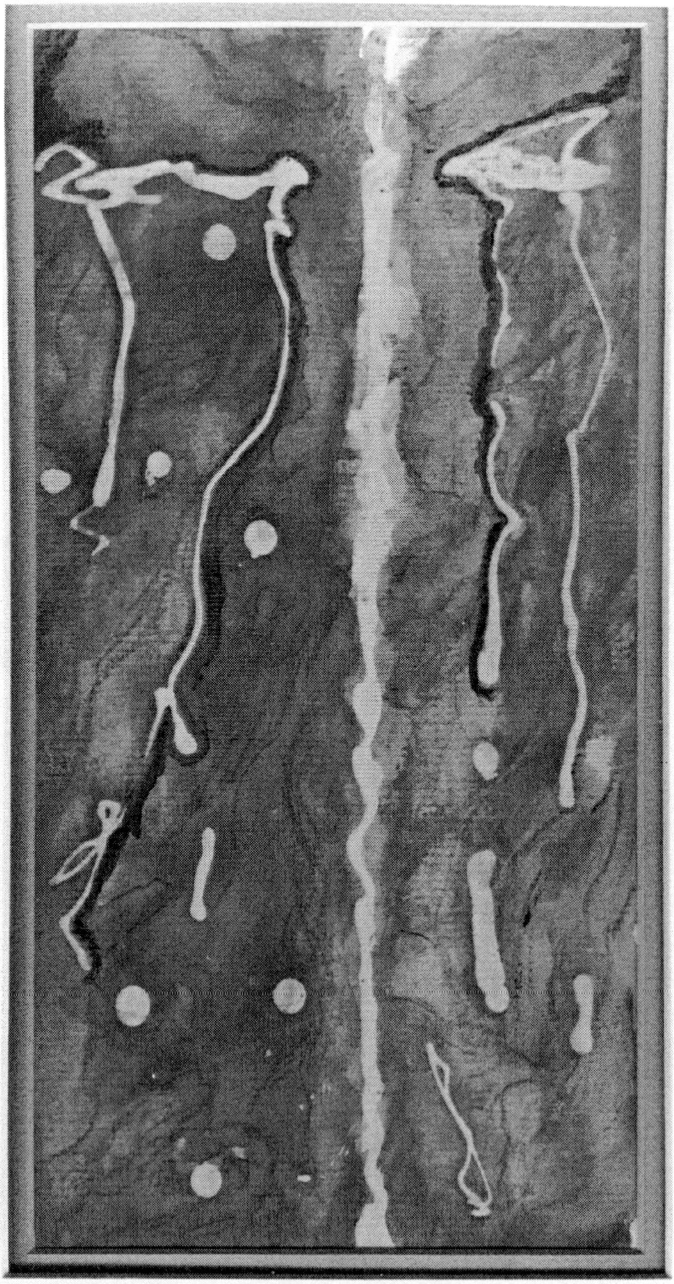

Hung Up Picture

CHAPTER 13

Care of Mother

The next dream points out how attending to what I call "Care of Mother" can impede my own progress. I am not talking about my actual mother, of course. She has been dead for many years. "Care of Mother" is a psychological state I fall into that is characterized by my impulses and desires being stifled without my really noticing, the state where I opt for comfort, no matter what it costs. Nothing's going to happen to me when I'm enjoying comfort.

MOTHER'S LOVE SEAT

> With several people, including my mother, I am running in the near-downtown area of my hometown. We're heading north and have two or three miles to go to our destination.
>
> My steps are light. I am bounding along without getting tired or winded. My springing steps take me ahead of the others so that I'm alone when I round a building and come upon a grassy plaza where four giant sycamore trees stand in a row across the area. Another stands alone some distance behind the row. Their leaves are yellow but have

not begun to fall, and the sun highlights their glory. I'm so stunned by the beauty of these trees that I stop and stare.

Now we have reached the place where my car is parked. I begin to load it up to go home.

Mother has been stopping in poor neighborhoods and picking up things at garage sales to bring home with us. Once she buys a love seat, which we then have to carry along awkwardly.

But now I have the task of loading the car, and I can't seem to do it. I try and try, but it doesn't get done. No one offers to help me, and I don't ask. One very tall man follows me, but instead of helping me load all this stuff, he puts his arms around me and holds me in a long hug.

Associations

LIGHT STEPS: Bounding along with springing steps is just short of flying. Plenty of spirit here! I am in the vicinity of my center, in the city, and heading for home. My steps are light enough to carry me out alone.

TREES: Trees of this quality in dreams are another symbol of connection with the divine, as tree-worshipping people knew centuries ago. Their trunks connect the deep roots (what is below) to the up reaching branches (what is above). Their massive size and their golden leaves make these trees seem beyond reality.

STUNNED: The moment of beholding this scene is a religious experience. I stand there stunned.

Then the moment of worship ends and I busy myself helping my mother stow her purchases in my car.

Perhaps it is significant that it is *my* car that we're using. Even though I don't want any of the things Mother has bought, they end up in my car. My own actual mother never had a car, never learned to drive; part of "Care of Mother" is carrying her in mine. And on "mother's love seat" there is only room for the two of us.

THE TALL MAN: This man, though his role in the present dream is small, will appear again and again later, as someone important. He doesn't serve my mother's interests, but rather the interests of our getting together. He is here to take me away from Mother and lead me on to the next phase of my life.

In one form or another, often as Vance himself, he has come many times before in my dreams, such as in this one:

THE MAN BEHIND ME

> I am traveling downward, a long, long way downward, first in a car going down several roads so steep I have to use the brake, then down a series of irregular steps. Some steps are only a few inches deep; others are a foot or more apart. As I go down, I sometimes walk, and I also run, and jump or spring down effortlessly.
>
> Now I become aware that all this time there has been a tall man close behind me. He walks when I walk, jumps when I jump, always staying right behind me, almost touching. I adjust my own movements slightly to synchronize with his.
>
> At the bottom of all the steps, he moves to my side and smiles at me. I say, "I'm so glad to see you!" I put my arm around him and we walk on.

LOVE SEAT: It is my *love* for my mother that stands in the way of separating from her and joining forces with the man. When I was in the throes of the childhood part of my soul journey, Mmmmm spent many hours in J's Magic Circle, envisioning what my early life must have seemed like to a small child. One of the most vivid scenes was this:

> I am a small child, younger than three years old. My parents are quarreling in the kitchen, quarreling about me. They begin to wrestle, and my father pushes Mother out the back door onto the porch. It is winter, and I am afraid

> she will freeze. I fly around the room, screaming for him to let her back in. I will do anything, anything, whatever it takes, to keep my mother from being kicked out.

That vow was very serious indeed. It was my mother I loved, and if keeping her meant keeping a lid on myself, then that was the price I would pay.

THE TASK: In this dream I am taking on the task of loading my mother's love seat into my car, and I can't get it done. This piece of furniture just won't fit. I cannot keep the chummy twosome of Mother and Child and still climb in my car and move along in the world.

How crucial this issue is for me became even more evident with the following dream:

HAVING TO LEAVE THE WRITING PROJECT

> I am away from home working on a writing project, staying in the house of a married couple. I had been staying with a different couple but had to leave because the man got too interested in me and I didn't want to be the cause of the woman's distress.
>
> Vance is the man of this new couple. They're fairly young. He does not treat her well. He's sharp with her, and impatient, as though she's not very bright and much too clinging and demanding.
>
> He treats me, however, like a devoted lover, finding reasons to spend time with me, taking part in my writing project. I accept and enjoy this without giving much thought to his wife.
>
> But now a weekend is coming up. I talk with the wife about plans and tell her that I'll work around whatever they've planned to do.
>
> She takes this as an opening. "As a matter of fact," she says, "sit down here and let's talk." I sit on a couch

where I am practically buried in pillows and bolsters. "Would you like some tea?" she asks nervously. I shake my head. "How about a blanket to wrap up in?" I shake my head again. With all the pillows around me, I couldn't possibly be cold.

She sits down nearby. I can see that she's really hurting. And then I realize what it is, that she is extremely threatened by Vance's interest in me. I will have to leave here. I can't stand to contribute to another woman's pain.

Associations

VANCE'S NEW WIFE: Here she is, a version of my mother, whose pain I cannot bear. Her solicitous treatment of me, offering comforts I don't need, brings back memories of my actual mother, the way we used to sit together and talk, sharing a blanket draped over the register to keep warm. All the pillows remind me of a dream fragment about my mother:

PILLOWY MOTHER

I am on a street corner, sitting on a bench. My mother is with me. She is very tired, so I hold her on my lap. She's very soft and not at all heavy, like a big down pillow, but I can't see around her.

HAVING TO LEAVE: Even though my writing project has the backing of a devoted lover, my buried but desperate old fear of mother's being kicked out is aroused by this woman's pain and I will sacrifice whatever it takes to protect her.

Needless to say, in my conscious life, I would (and did) choose Vance, but this is happening to me outside my field of awareness.

So what can I do?

What I have actually been doing about this is to notice the quiet whisper of internal conversation that comes up when I feel an impulse to do something. "Not now," she will say. "Sit down. Have some nice hot tea instead."

And then I must summon the strength to override that voice and push myself to do whatever my impulse was.

The voice always sounds helpful, not critical or cruel. To pull me away from my impulses, it offers me tea, a blanket, pillows, comforts, pleasure. It's very hard to get angry at, hard to talk back to.

I finally took the step of writing to my mother, starting in the form of a letter, but ending with a fully visualized and heartbreaking scene:

> Dear Mother,
>
> Much as I appreciate your help and enjoy your presence, it is time for you to go now. Time to leave me on my own.
>
> I could not say this any sooner because I was still committed to keeping you close, assuring that you weren't kicked out. But your presence here now has a deadening effect on me, as though you were a parasite sucking the juice out of me.
>
> You have a place elsewhere, with your friends, coworkers, your sisters, all the people who loved you, whose lives you enhanced by the quality of your interest and attention. You must go to them now and leave me alone. This house arranged by images requires a single focus, not the blur of double vision.
>
> So out the door with you. Here's your coat, your purse, your hat. The bus stop is two blocks down the hill.
>
> Now stand up straight and don't look pitiful. Think of this as your chance too, your chance not to miss the bus this time around.

Showing my mother the door after the years of mighty efforts I've made to keep her from being kicked out was a powerful envisioning accompanied by strong emotion and followed by the question: What's going to happen now?

The first thing that happened was an attack of great wretchedness in my back, shoulders, and ribs that comes upon me without a cause that I'm conscious of, such as a strain or twist. It can lay me low and tempt me into a library book binge and, of course, I usually give in. This time I suspected retaliation by the complex and instead of lying on the heating pad reading comforting Brother Cadfael mysteries, I visited both the chiropractor and the massage therapist and returned to my studio.

And I stuck to my impulse-following regimen. "Respond right away to the impulse," J suggested, because the complex begins to dampen it immediately, whispering spirit-killing messages such as:

- Wait till later.
- It won't work out.
- It's too much trouble.
- Do this other thing first, or this, or this.
- It will make a mess and you'll have to clean it up.
- You won't have the energy to keep going with it anyway.
- Why not just sit back and take it easy?

And sometimes the complex doesn't even whisper: it immobilizes me without a word.

And then there was the single-image dream:

MY MOTHER WANTS TO ADOPT ME

There she was, putting out feelers, needing me. Finally came the following:

THE WARNING

> I am living at Vance's house again after being away for a long time. I notice a door in the kitchen and remember with pleasure that it leads to the basement.

Now I'm shopping at a produce stand. The aisles are crowded with shoppers. I've chosen several items, and I do a kind of "after you, no after you" dance with another woman, finding a place to put them aside while I look for something else.

The produce is beautiful, especially a new variety of cauliflower that has a flat disk of a head with a rosy center.

In talking with the people here I mention that I'm going to be away for a few days staying with my mother.

Now I go to gather up my selections, but I can't find them. I look all around, but they aren't here. Everything is disorganized.

Associations

VANCE'S HOUSE: As an inner place, this is the Lover's house, and it is a long way from Wallflower Woman's house. In HAVING TO LEAVE THE WRITING PROJECT I left Vance's house because of my fear of distressing the other wife, but now I'm back where I belong.

KITCHEN: The place where nourishment is prepared. The door to the basement is right at hand. The kitchen in the Lover's house is a soul kitchen where something rich and satisfying is always cooking.

J. E. Cirlot's *A Dictionary of Symbols* says: "The kitchen, since this is where foodstuff is transformed, sometimes signifies the place or the moment of psychic transmutation in the alchemical sense."[11] To transform the details of one's dream life into a story is like making a black walnut cake from the broken kernels of childhood.

FOOD: The rosy-centered cauliflower has qualities that make it seem more symbolic than material, nourishment for the soul rather than the body.

Of all the hundreds of dreams I've had about food and cooking, the one that sums up the symbolism best is this one:

11. *A Dictionary of Symbols* by J. E. Cirlot, Philosophical Library

LOAVES AND FISHES

> I have been given a recipe for the loaves and the fishes. It is jotted down casually on the cover of the poetry chapbook LOAVES AND FISHES, some of the ingredients listed under LOAVES and some under FISHES.

This poetry chapbook, edited by Alice Friman, is an anthology of women's poems, and it includes a poem of mine. A poetry-book recipe for the loaves and the fishes has to be for the soul food of imagination and language. Wasn't it soul food, after all, that Jesus fed the multitudes?

PRODUCE STAND: One of my favorite places, where you buy choice fruits and vegetables that go into the nourishment prepared in the kitchen. There may be a play on words here too, produce-the-noun being garden products, and produce-the-verb being to create or make something. By visiting this place I come to a new product, the beautiful new cauliflower. The shape and appearance of this vegetable, a flat disk with a rosy center, leads me to interpret it as another symbol of divinity, like a rose window in a cathedral.

VISITING MOTHER: But here's the warning. It's much too easy to slip back into a visit with Mother, much too easy to be lured onto her love seat with pillows and cups of tea, where everything is easy, comfortable, and safe, not too unlike an expensive nursing home. No mosquitoes here!

Quote of the Day expressed the situation this way: "The lust for comfort, that stealthy thing that enters the house a guest, then becomes a host, and then a master," from *The Prophet*, "On Houses," by Kahlil Gibran.

Indeed, everything falls apart as I mention the visit. I can no longer find my rosy-centered cauliflower, nor anything else to take home for our nourishment.

CHAPTER 14

Remodeling

ALL BUT THE BATHROOM

I am in my parents' house, which is being greatly remodeled. My dad is doing the work, and he's cheerful about it, as though it's giving him pleasure.

Several small children are here with boxes of toys that they drag around from place to place and play with.

I go upstairs. The steps are now white and marbled with gray; they need sweeping. The bathroom has not been worked on yet. The fake tile wall covering is blue and battered. I go in and hook the door, telling the children that I'm going to be in here a while. There's a pile of newspaper and magazine clippings on the floor. I select one to read while I'm on the pot. It is titled "Success."

Associations

HOUSE BEING REMODELED: Work being done on one's childhood home implies change in some long-standing psychological way of being. This dream is only one of several recent ones with this theme, no doubt a result of all the work I've done.

CHILDREN AND THEIR TOYS: Here the children are playing with toys while the house is being remodeled. My father is in a good mood, quite unlike I remember him being when I was a child. This image of the children and their toys requires a reference to another, earlier dream:

AND NEVER GO NEAR HIM AGAIN

> I'm a child in this dream. I'm in an unfamiliar place among strangers. My father is here too, and he's sick, lying on the couch, maybe with a fever.
>
> Now he's standing up, acting very odd, like someone else, or like in an altered state. He presses me close and whispers to me. He kisses me like a lover. He seems like a zombie — he's unaffected by anything I do, and he won't let go. But after a long time I finally escape from him.
>
> I never go near him again, ever.
>
> Some of the people here have toys that they pass around to the children. I'm suspicious. I won't take a toy. I know it will just be snatched away. I see other children taking toys, but I won't do it.

Comments

Toys are there for the taking, but my suspicion will not allow me any. This dream implies that whatever rubbed off from my father's embrace resulted in a reduced ability to believe in the trustworthiness of toys or other good things.

My father was not demonstrative, and I have no memory of ever being held or kissed by him at all, but the dream was correct in stating that I would never go near him again. I didn't. I stayed well away from him. He looked upon me with a jealous eye, and this did not draw me close.

He continued to be jealous of me until the end of his life. He came to my bedroom door once when I was napping, banged on the door and yelled, "Who's in there with you?" Even though he was a helpless old man at the time and I the married daughter taking care of him, this intrusion terrified me.

But recently, after much psychological work, his image has been changing in my dreams. And he's been working on remodeling.

CHEERFUL: Imagine (without trying to believe) that the dead still exist on some level. Suppose they still care. I like to imagine their better selves cheering us on as we repair damage from the past. Wouldn't my father be pleased at what I'm doing if his better self were privy to what's going on? Maybe as I revise my own attitude, his gets some help too. Maybe his cheerfulness in the dream is about changing that attitude.

GOING UPSTAIRS: Moving to a higher, more intellectual or spiritual level. The dirt on the floor, of course, is still the part that never gets resolved, that can't be tidied up neatly or explained, the seeds of the next step. Going upstairs could refer to ascending to a plane where there can be thinking and insight about the matters at hand, rather than the pure feeling or the pure instinct of lower levels. It's like looking through the upstairs window in FINDING MY OWN MUSIC.

THE BATHROOM: This is the place where people attend to their most personal and intimate needs. These needs always bear consideration when a dream is set in the bathroom.

For me, a person of the generation of very early and manipulated toilet training, the bathroom has particular layers of significance, having to do with the thwarting of natural, impulsive expression. This is the room that still needs work. Maybe it always will.

SUCCESS: At the time of this dream, I had just finished a large section of this book and handed it to J to read, hoping that he would add his insight to what I had written. But after I came home, something unusual took me over and I ended up getting drunk sipping the Jamaica rum I was using to season the black beans I had cooked for dinner.

Getting drunk is something that had not happened to me for many years, not since my younger, partying days, and the significance of this event was not lost on me.

I realized that I was *afraid* of J's reaction to my manuscript, his *envious* reaction to my success. He too had a manuscript he was working on, and he too had trouble with it from time to time. Just as I was afraid of being rejected by the images for taking on too much territory for myself, I was afraid of being rejected by J for muscling into his field, that of writing about dreams. After all, he was the therapist and I the client. Who did I think I was, writing such a manuscript?

When I talked with J about all this later, he admitted that he had indeed felt some envy, but he thought that my getting drunk was more likely to be related to my skepticism, my inability to trust the Spirit in the images to stay with me. "A powerful *spirited response* to your skepticism," he said. Imbibing spirits is an attempt to become inspirited.

My skepticism speaks with the voice of my father. It is responsible for the words *nothing butta* and is reductionist in the extreme, as illustrated by the following dream:

REDUCING A FULL GLASS

> I'm outdoors at a picnic table with several people nearby. On the table are two or three jugs. The liquid in one of them has separated into a gold-colored layer and a clear one. I shake the jug but do not pour.
>
> Now I have a glass of liquid, a large glass with about ten ounces in it. I point my finger at the liquid. It retreats under my pointing finger and reduces to a third its original volume, about three ounces.
>
> The people around me think I am performing a parlor trick, but I'm not. I don't know how it happened. I try to do it again, this time using a glass of bubbly seltzer water. With the bubbly water, my pointing finger has no effect.

Comments

If a ten ounce glass had five ounces of liquid in it, one could see it as either half full or half empty, but when ten ounces of liquid are reduced to three by merely pointing at it, that is reductionism of a high order.

Notice that only the liquid without bubbles (without Spirit) can be reduced this way, however. When the Spirit is present, my skeptic finger is not effective. Notice also that I pay no attention to the gold-colored liquid in the jug. When I'm in Reductionist Mode, I do not recognize the value of what is present.

The situation with my father seems to be improving in the following dream:

A HUG AND A SMILE AT LAST

My father is here looking grouchy and unapproachable. But I approach him anyway. I touch him and say, "I don't like it that we're always on the outs." He breaks into a wonderful smile and opens his arms. We hug warmly. I have never had a hug like that from my father before.

I don't know where things are kept here. Mother seems to be nearby, and maybe I could ask her, but I don't see her. I am looking for the spices to do some cooking. Finally I find them in a cupboard hidden behind a panel of curved plastic.

Now I am outdoors arranging a bench to sit on against the trunk of a massive tree. The ground is uneven, with a drop-off alongside, so it takes several tries, but at last I settle the bench on a fairly stable ledge and sit down with my back leaning against the tree. Someone else is nearby, and we talk.

I hear someone saying that her work has been influenced by T. S. Eliot's poems.

Associations

THE HUG: I didn't know I wanted a hug from my father, but when it came, it was wonderful. He did indeed have a nice smile, with twinkling blue eyes and good teeth, but during my childhood, he didn't use it very often.

SPICES: These are the spices that give flavor to life, no doubt, and in a home with my parents and their cautionary approach, the spices would be hard to find. They certainly weren't out in a spice rack for easy use. I do find them, however, and that's a good sign.

THE TREE: Another image of the divine, rooted deeply in the earth and reaching heavenward. My place here is still shaky, but I'm able to lean.

SOMEONE: When I lead imaginative writing workshops, I often ask participants to write for ten or fifteen minutes, starting with the words, "Someone wants to say..." This "someone" is an unrecognized part of me who has something to tell me.

T. S. ELIOT: Eliot's poem, "The Wasteland," perhaps. When I began working with J, he asked me what I was most afraid of. I replied without a moment's hesitation that I was afraid of wasting my life. My motivation in doing this work is to avoid the fate of Mrs. Linton in the nursing home with the emerald star hidden in her mattress, too late to dance.

The next dream belongs here too, having a scene of remodeling:

TOTAL IMMERSION

1. My old writing teacher does not recognize me in a crowd. I am unwilling to leave without being seen. There are so many other people around him that they form a barrier. I push them out of the way, even stabbing a few with something sharp. My teacher watches in his intent way of noticing incongruities. When we are face to face, he tells me that I look familiar, but he doesn't remember who I am.

2. I am soaking wet, water running out of my hair, and all I have to put on is my red jacket. I wrap up in it as best I can, and I ornament my streaming wet hair with a round flat disk of thin rubber, pulling a lock of hair through a hole in it. I'm seated at a table waiting for something. All of my belongings have been taken away from me. I have nothing left except for the red jacket I'm wearing.

3. The house I grew up in has been undergoing renovation. The whole back has been remodeled. The porches are gone. New white paint gleams richly in the sunlight. The paint looks thick and soft, as though it would be resilient to the touch. The house is much larger than I remember, and without the porches it seems very tall. I decide to plant a tree to soften the appearance of this immense expanse of white.

Associations

BEING SEEN: There's more to being seen than being looked at, a deeper recognition and thus more of a connection. Being-looked-at sees the surface, but being-seen sees who you really are.

This image harks back to FINDING MY OWN MUSIC in several ways. When I am part of the Collective, when I am in the crowd, I am not being authentic, and thus I cannot connect with the inner writer. To be seen by him I have to push, I even have to stab through the crowd with something sharp. He says I look familiar, but he doesn't know who I am. I am sharper and more eccentric than I was when he knew me.

This inner writing teacher is essential to me because he's a writer who stands firmly with his own idiosyncrasies. And his interest is necessary because he's the one with the energy and the discipline to get the work done.

Indeed, I have noticed that my energy flags when I try to be fair, considerate, nice or politically correct in my writing. And it flows when I write sharply, devoting myself to presenting the images as clearly and truthfully as possible.

WET: I have obviously just emerged from under the water.

When J and I talked about this image, we had no premonition that within a few hours another immersion would occur that would alter everything. All unbeknownst we talked happily about the *solutio* of alchemy and its similarity to Christian baptism, where one comes out of the water reborn. Reborn, perhaps, as someone sharper, more eccentric, and much less nice than I once was.

NOTHING LEFT BUT THE RED GARMENT: I felt vulnerable with only the red jacket to cover my nakedness, but also remembered the red dress that had been torn off me as a child and what it implied. Red being the color of the life force, wearing the jacket while being relieved of all my other belongings seems even more like a rebirth, a fresh start.

RUBBER DISK: This piece of soft rubber was like two household items: a drain stopper and a jar opener. I use the disk to adorn my head and hold a lock of hair in place, protecting my mental processes from either draining out or being stuck shut.

WHITE HOUSE: The place is so large and impressive that it looks almost presidential. That's more remodeling than I expected.

J noticed the word "resilient" about the paint, something that springs back or recovers, as from misfortune. How I will need this resiliency in the months to come!

TREE: As I reflected upon this dream, I remembered that it had been the picture of a tree that was the beginning of my move to the Pacific Northwest. I had been leafing through a literary magazine and noticed an ad with a tree logo on it from the Centrum Foundation offering subsidized residencies for writers at Fort Worden State Park on the Olympic Peninsula. I applied, was accepted, spent two months there, and subsequently left Indiana to move nearby. I imagine the tree pictured as one of Fort Worden's lindens, which are handsome spreading trees that bloom profusely with a sweet perfume. They attract a multitude of bees that you can hear in concerted buzzing as you approach the trees in early July.

This tree is one of many in my dreams, several of them mentioned here. It's another of the symbols of the divine. To plant such a tree would be a work worth doing.

That was the last time I saw J. When the afternoon meeting had ended, he left a "Back in time for dinner" note for his wife and went out in his kayak into the waters off Point Wilson where the Strait of Juan de Fuca opens into Admiralty Inlet, the entrance to Puget Sound. Beach walkers saw his kayak in trouble in rough water. The Coast Guard searched for him all night. The next morning the kayak washed up, and in the evening his body was found.

I am only one of the many persons to grieve this terrible accident. A number of the others are friends of mine. His work touched people deeply.

But each of us struggles with this death on a personal basis, each with a fantasy of how it went for him at the end and what it means for the ones who are left. In our many talks about what is real and what is important, he often used the phrase, "My fantasy is..." About his death *my* fantasy is that he had time there in the water to meet his death with courage and the same integrity he had shown in life, to think of all of us, and to bequeath what he could leave behind. My fantasy is that *my* portion of his bequest was the trust and the faith to carry on with the soul work that both of us saw as vital.

Some weeks later I wrote to Mmmmm:

Me: It must be hard for you not having J any longer.

Mmmmm: It would be hard if that were true, but he only left you behind. He didn't leave me

After I had absorbed that surprising bit of information I asked her:

Me: Are you still encased in your not-here prison?

Mmmmm: No. I have wings now, but they are still wet.

Me: Are you still afraid of being collected or sprayed?

Mmmmm: Right now, that is not my biggest concern. Right now I am wondering if my wings are going to be big and strong enough to carry me. I am a big moth with furry legs and a big furry body, not a butterfly. I need big strong wings.

Me: Can you spread your wings out to dry?

Mmmmm: Yes, I can do that, but the breeze has to help too.

Me: I will look for breezy places.

Mmmmm: That would be nice.

Later, however, Mmmmm began to realize that J was *really* gone. Her heartbreak came through when this appeared in her notebook:

Mmmmm says: When he went into the water, he folded up the Magic Circle and took it with him. It's gone now, and so is he.

PART 4

In the Depths

CHAPTER 15

The Gods

I did not engage in the massive turmoil of uprooting myself from my lifelong Indiana home and moving to the Pacific Northwest for the usual reasons: the mountains, the water, the climate, the ambiance, although I certainly enjoy these benefits. With help and support from Vance, I came specifically to enter the process described in these pages: soul work. Within two months of my arrival I had met J, joined his dream group and began seeing him privately as well.

In the months before his death the private sessions were getting fewer and farther apart, with much less wretchedness to work through. But having J's guidance come to such an abrupt and grievous end led me to take stock of where I stood in the work.

The process had been strenuous. One doesn't realize, beginning it, just what it means to face one's inner conflicts and the images they present. For most of us these conflicts are as intractable as the outer necessities of economic survival and social adaptation. The commitment required to do this work, the energy, comes close to what it takes to raise a child, or participate in an intense marriage, or earn an advanced degree, all of which I know something about. I described the inner journey in this poem:

WHERE MOUNTAINS RISE OUT OF THE SOUND[12]

Sometimes I see a woman here
Who left her home to settle
Where mountains rise out of the Sound.
This woman is becoming the Olympic Peninsula.
A hard road pierces the interior.
A steep road, mud and stones.
A single wind uproots a thousand firs.
In one a cat clings through the storm to the uppermost branch.
When the tree blows down, she knows something new about her claws.
On the beach, a gale throws sand like powder.
Scours the weeping bluff above.
Finally the face leans out, groans, and falls.
You stand back then.
Cover your ears.
Wait.
The road inward washes away.
So much water.
So much water.
Mist and moss hang quiet on the west slope.
A new perfume like salt.
She nurses logs.
This is the place for her best stand.

It is important not only to take a stand on life, but to take one's *best* stand, in order to live with meaning and attend to what has value. What that stand is will depend on a number of factors: the DNA, the native tongue, the physical strengths and weaknesses, the personal history, the community resources. The other factor that is important is one's psychic make up: who the inner characters are and how they behave.

12. "Where Mountains Rise Out of the Sound" was published in *The Flying Island* by the Writers' Center Press.

One way a person builds an identity is by serving the gods. A person who doesn't know who she is or where she lives can find out soon enough by noticing which gods she serves, and how. Taking one's best stand means attending to one's most troublesome gods as well as one's most venerated.

Then comes the question: which gods are they? How can a person find out? It isn't a matter of looking through a sacred text or a mythology book, finding a god or goddess that seems attractive, and deciding to worship that one. It's more a matter of being hounded by one or another of them through recurring images and thoughts, or worse, through annoying and unpleasant symptoms, compulsions and sicknesses, which are the more obnoxious manifestations of a deity.

One of the gods who pursues me is Hermes. An early appearance of Hermes in my life might have been as the instigator of the dream I had as a six year old being taught the word "communication," since Hermes is the messenger god of communication, as well as of thievery and trickery. His presence may account for my being a conduit of images from the unconscious realm into consciousness. He invented the lyre, and he was a swift runner with wings on his hat and his heels, thus he was honored by both musicians and athletes. The hot young man who tried to drag me away from the chorus in FINDING MY OWN MUSIC, which ends with the lyrebirds hung up on the line, might well have been following the dictate of Hermes.

A dream that seems to come from a different deity is the following:

PERFORCE

> My computer shifts suddenly out of the word processing program into one I know nothing about, except that it's called "Perforce." Displayed on the monitor is a metal grid surrounded by a metal frame. The horizontal cables of the grid attach to the frame with tightly coiled springs.

Several flat metal plates are strung on each cable at irregular intervals. These pieces are etched with mysterious symbols.

This is a picture of what underlies our reality.

Now there's another shift. The picture is no longer on the monitor; it has become real, a scene through the window. The grid is huge, taking up the entire sky. A man, dwarfed to ant-size by his surroundings, climbs laboriously on the grid.

Associations

PERFORCE: This seldom-used word means "by necessity" or "by force of circumstances," and it led me to think that the dream went beyond talking about my computer. Necessity is one of the deities: Ananke, the Greek Fate-goddess, who hammers out the chains of destiny that bind both gods and humans. Ananke carries a hammer, and when we feel the hammering of our fate upon us, hear the clanking of its chains, then through our suffering we become more willing to put aside our worldly pursuits and try to extract meaning from that fate.

REALITY: With many years of empiricism, pragmatism, and rational humanist thinking behind me, I have usually viewed such dreams as PERFORCE as interesting curiosities rather than insights into a different dimension of reality.

But both the symbolic and the material exist and are necessary. This dream suggests that the material world rests upon the symbolic. Since in mainstream thinking such a view is so overpowered by its opposite, I feel that the dream calls me to lend my weight to the symbolic view, to do my part to bring about a balance.

An early dream urging me into polytheism is this one:

WHICH GOD?

I have learned through trial and error that I must be precise when I ask the gods for anything, to ask for each specific benefit from the appropriate god.

The error I made in learning this was when I asked for and got a little square of something from the wrong god. This mistake brought noisy derision down on me from the others. But I get another chance, because that time was just a trial run.

Comments

My religious upbringing was monotheistic, and so was most of my thinking for many years, assuming that all things occurred in and through the Judeo-Christian God.

But the truth of God's oneness could not be demonstrated. I entered a long period of atheism, when all the old dogmas about God came into question and failed the test. Then I began to wonder, not how true my beliefs were but how useful. Since I could not attest to the *truth* of any way of thinking, I needed a way that was *useful*.

That one could think psychologically, rather than religiously, about gods was wonderfully useful. My reading led me into the possibility that one can see gods as metaphors for psychic forces that seize us against our will, rather than believe in the literal reality of one or more gods. Polytheism allowed me to separate one feeling from another, one train of thought, one cluster of images, one inner person. Instead of everything being stirred into confusion, things became much more clear. My Ego was no longer King of the World. I was no longer responsible for every emotion that washed over me, every image that showed up in my mind's eye, and thus I could take more responsibility for acting in ways that were possible about the things that *were* my responsibility. No longer did I have to try desperately not to *feel* the way I felt but some other, more agreeable, way. No longer did I have to try to change Mmmmm's way of being; I could relate to her as she actually was. What a relief!

Now, when a dream image seems to relate to a particular god, I try to flesh the image out by learning something about how that god manifested in other times and places, its lineage and progeny, its deeds. This research adds to the richness of the image and gives clues about what the god is trying to do with me. It works in much the same way as checking the etymology of a word, discovering where the word has been and how used, who its relatives are and what kind of reputation it has. Research of this kind is soul satisfying. It serves no purpose in the marketplace, but it feeds the deep hunger for conscious connection.

With such a reward for attention to the gods, it is easy to lean toward a bit of worship. Like the process theologians, who maintain that the monotheistic God of the Christians, Jews and Muslims is in a continual state of being created and needs our help, I wonder if it might not be appropriate to help the multitude of specialty gods as well.

A dream that specifies one of the specialty gods is the following:

AION

> Art pieces are being returned from a show. I get back a portrait of a wizard holding a sheet of paper. I had forgotten about painting this picture, but now I remember modeling the wizard's face after a bas-relief of the god Aion that is on the wall above. I'm pleased that this painting is so well done.
>
> A group of us are living apart from the rest of society while working on something of the utmost importance. Sometimes we get discouraged about our work.
>
> Now one of the men in the group tacks up a proclamation on the door, something so wise that the value of our undertaking is immediately evident. Our faith in the work is then restored.

Associations

AION: The ancient Greek word "aion" refers to time as an age or an eternity. It has the Mithraic Time-god Aion behind it, and this god's face is on my painting: a lion's face. My using this face under a wizard's hat in my painting implies something about the subject of the paper he is holding, probably religious, probably wise. This paper might well be the proclamation that is tacked up on the door at the end of my dream.

UTMOST IMPORTANCE: If I were to make this claim of "utmost importance" while awake, with my puffed-up Ego strutting, it would have to be taken as pretentious. But the Ego is not the source of dream images. I am being *told* that the work is important, not *claiming* that it is.

To whom, I wonder. Certainly not to any of the usual judges. But just as Wall Street is convinced of its own importance, so, perhaps, should Psyche be.

At the very least, this work is important because it demonstrates that there is another game in town besides the mirror and the mall.

PROCLAMATION: Tacking a proclamation on the door in a dream like this brings up thoughts of Martin Luther, who nailed his ninety-five theses to the door of the castle church in Wittenberg, thus beginning the Protestant Reformation.

The reader must not conclude that working with the gods is a completely solemn process. Some of the funniest dreams I've had are images (or voices) from on high.

One of these voices was the deep, sonorous voice of God, which spoke in a consoling way, telling me:

BEAN JOYS

There will always be bean joys: knots on the suspenders
of what holds you up.

I took this to mean that my sense of humor would stand me in good stead even while I was in the depths of depression.

The same voice informed me about the errors of scripture in:

GENESIS

Genesis is wrong. It all began with a purple dog.

This image resulted in the fanciful picture on the next page.

And then came:

THE WRATH OF GOD

A garbage truck rumbles past. In the pile of garbage I see a head sticking out, a head with long white hair and an angry face. A fist emerges. Then I see the legs sticking out as well. There are no feet attached to the legs. I recognize this as the Wrath of God.

Comments

I did not grow up with the common image of God as a squad car, but seeing the footless Wrath being hauled away to the dump was not unpleasant.

Is a compelling image a message from wherever the gods reside? Sometimes dream images seem urgent, as though panting to be expressed. Such an image in a dream of mine was that of a window on which a red leaf had been plastered by a storm. The following poem was the result:

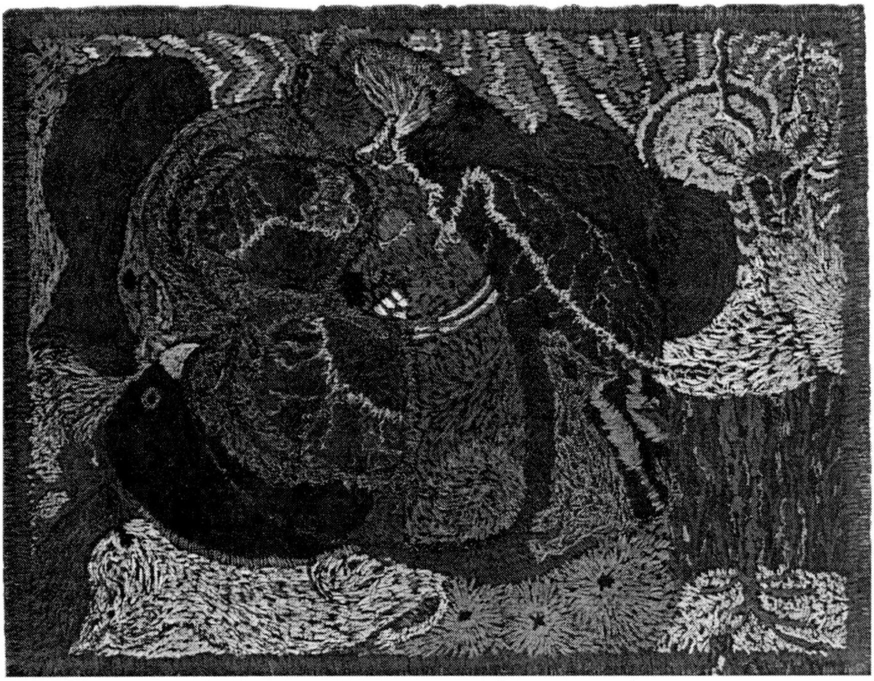

Purple Dog

WINDOW WITH A RED LEAF[13]

On a day well past the halfway point of life
I climb the stairs to watch it rain
through wavy glass at the top of the house.
The window is so high I cannot reach
the clasp to swing it open. Sitting dry, I watch
the clouds puff by, feeling with my eye the gusts
that make the most of every drop of small
rain hurtling through the autumn sky.
Another nonproductive way to pass
an afternoon that won't contribute
to my résumé or reputation, like
mindful breathing in a steady line
in and out for some unmeasured length of time.
Or peeling an apple in one long
strip of red and yellow without a break,
or piling beach rocks in a cairn the tide will take.
But I am drawn to these pursuits by forces
much too muscular to cross, and thus
I let myself be beckoned up
like a sky-pulled oak to the stormy
theater of blue and gray and white clouds,
to see the roused wet western wind strike
tears upon the single attic eye
in the forehead of my house.
I've been brought to watch a red leaf
smack against the glass and stick,
to smell the curl of wood smoke
trickling like memory of old fire
through a long crack in the window frame.
"Needs caulk," I hear my father say.

13. "Windown with a Red Leaf" was published in *The Flying Island* by the Writers' Center Press

I make another useless mental note,
and take another breath of fragrant smoke.

One morning when I was feeling poorly after my knee surgery, I wrote in my journal how much I missed mobility, energy, being able to enjoy luxuries, etc. Suddenly my whining turned into a conversation between two inner entities:

First Voice: Who will speak for the values of pain, illness, debilitation, misery and death? These are part of life too, but no one praises them.

Second Voice: Don't expect a human voice to speak for such values. Humans identify with their bodies, which are made of the same stuff as their surroundings and are subject to the same laws. But unlike their inanimate surroundings, humans have the capacity to notice the grinds and crashes of the material world. H_2O does not cry out when it changes from ice to steam, but humans do. Because of the pain involved, they do not value the changes.

Me: Who are you?

Second Voice: A mediator. A translator. My kind move between the temporal and the eternal, between the material and the spiritual realms. We carry the sensate experience of creatures into the eternal world, and we bring the knowledge of the eternal to humans.

I am the one who comes when you call. I feed you little bites of spirit toast, little mouthfuls of wisdom. Where do you think ideas come from? Do you think that you are the creator of the word? I feed you words and ideas and images.

Me: Spirit toast indeed!

Mmmmm says: Butter please, if we're having toast.

CHAPTER 16

Death

In *Re-Visioning Psychology* James Hillman writes about soul and its relationship with death. The guided part of my soul work, the wrestling, was done with J, who has now died. My anger at him for his reckless dying cannot be part of the dialogue, as it certainly would have been if he had survived. Nor can I tell him what a loss I feel. He doesn't answer my complaints and accusations. He does not hear out my grief with sympathy. His death was not part of our dialogue, but it is part of our relationship and part of my soul work.

My husband's death contributed to my decision to put this manuscript together, and so did the death of the sexual assault survivor support program I worked for. The introspection required to do the job would not have been possible as long as my attention was directed outward. I'm not being Panglossian here, assigning value to these deaths, saying it was all for the best in this "best of all possible worlds," only remarking that in my case solitude filled itself with industry.

What follows is the text of a short "thankfulness" talk I presented as one of three speakers at a Thanksgiving service at Quimper Unitarian-Universalist Fellowship:

Eulogy

One Thanksgiving, when Vance had been dead for only three months, I went to my studio in the morning to write. After a while I noticed the odor of cigarette smoke. Since no one, not even Vance, had ever smoked in my studio, I knew it couldn't be lingering odor on the furniture. I walked around sniffing for hot cords, but there weren't any, and besides, it was *cigarette* smoke that I smelled. I realized then that either I was having an olfactory hallucination or this was a visitation from Vance. Just in case it was the latter, I dashed in the house and turned on the TV, knowing he would want to watch the Thanksgiving football game. I even apologized to him for not having any beer on hand.

This is all to say that Vance was as aggravating as most men: he watched football and he drank beer and he smoked himself to death, and it's to say that it isn't because he was a saint that I am thankful for the almost thirty years that I knew him. "I don't know why I put up with you," I told him once, and he slitted his eyes at me and answered, "It's because I'm the best you can do." And he was.

Almost thirty years. I don't know when we actually met. My Great Books group was in its third or fourth year, and his group had dwindled down to five or six people and so they joined forces with us. I remember him as being articulate and brilliant and thoughtful and funny, and I was always interested in what he had to say. He was completely frank about what he thought, how he felt, what he saw. He was so outspoken that many people avoided him, in spite of his warmth and charm and generosity, because he had a nose for pompous bullshit and he didn't hesitate to say so when he smelled it. I remember one of our members had a habit of referring every topic back to the ancients and Vance once told him he was an intellectual necrophiliac. But because he was so frank and also so thoughtful, people came to him for an honest opinion, and he built close friendships throughout his life, even at the very end.

It wasn't until several years later that we had anything in common besides being members of the Great Books group and the Unitarian Church. I had started writing by that time and was back in college finishing up my undergraduate work. Then some people at church started a literary magazine, and I submitted a story. As it happened, Vance was editing the fiction for the magazine and was moved by the story, which was then published. Up until then, he hadn't really known there was any more to me than what showed in my roles as hostess of good parties, Unitarian, and Great Books member. But from then on, he was interested, and he sought me out more and more often.

When Vance was growing up, he used to mosey downtown to the art institute on Saturdays. He was not an artist himself but he liked going to the museum. What really came to interest him, though, was the art process itself, much more than the finished product. In fact, he was so intrigued by the process that he got impatient with the products and all the hype that went on around them. I've heard him say more than once that all art ought to self-destruct after twenty years to make room for the new.

So one of the things that interested him about me was an art process in its early stages. I was writing stories and poems and he was reading them, and we would talk. He pushed me to become conscious of what I was writing and to go deeper. We took walks in the botanical garden and on the grounds of the old mansion where the new museum of art was being built and we talked some more.

Well, as anyone with a grain of sense could figure, we fell in love. This presented problems. We were both married to fine people, and neither of us treated our partners and our commitments in a casual way. But as it happened they were already noticing and talking with each other about it, and they got interested in each other too. It took several years for all of this to happen, but in the end my husband and I separated, I took the girls and left the state to go to graduate school. Vance and his wife also separated and his wife moved in with my husband. This left Vance alone for two years, but he had a car and he used it. He drove 385 miles after work every Friday to visit me and drove back home on Sunday. When I finished my degree, I considered that I had been adequately courted, and that he was trustworthy and of good character, and the girls and I moved in with him. Eventually, after several more years we all got divorced and remarried to make the actual state of affairs legal.

As you can imagine, none of this was easy. We were all concerned with preserving what was valuable, with making a good environment for each of us as well as for the children involved, the youngest of whom was now fourteen. But we all had the usual emotions, too, so our family activities took on some of the aspects of a long-running soap opera. You ought to hear what the seven kids have to say when some occasion brings them back together for reminiscing.

What kept us going through all that and through everything else that happened over the years was that what we had together was the real thing. It was as though a perfectly ordinary couple was blessed with an extraordinary love. People get gifts, like beauty or intelligence or talent or faith. We got the gift of love.

This is not to say he didn't bring other gifts to me and I to him. He brought his interest in visual art, which I had never noticed before, being primarily sound and feeling oriented. He brought knowledge about and interest in political science and government. I brought a deeper involvement with literature and more insight into people than he was used to, as well as making a warm and comfortable home. But the love that enfolded us was the important thing.

It carried us through the soap opera and then it carried us through buying a big house and moving his demented mother and my demented father in to take care of, along with teenagers and pets. It came with us when he retired and we sold the big house and gave all the family heirlooms to the kids and moved here to the Olympic Peninsula to live an entirely different life. And it carried us through the year and a half of illness that preceded his death.

Because I was writing all the time this was going on, I have a great many poems and stories that mark this process and I'd like to read you two of the poems.

The first one is from the period when we had a house full of people to take care of and a lot of chores we didn't want to do. I had never been able to write soupy love stuff, and I asked him if this would suffice as a love poem. He said it sounded like a *constancy* poem to him.

ABOUT THE FEET[14]

Those feet,
their heels upholstered in fine sandpaper
file away at my probing toenails
down by the footboard
nights.

The feet know each other,
know where the others come from—
are going—
all four with arches like de Triomphe and thin skin.
They war frequently:
heels flail
and nails peel off old mosquito bite scabs
but through the years in the bed together
the soles support
unscarred.

Things, however, are not the same
up at the top
where we keep books on how to preserve
and Kleenex because nothing is ever preserved
and a clock to prove how long he has to wait for me
or I for him.

When we wake up,
sometimes he tells me in lengthy approximations
how he feels about something important,
and because I already know how he feels
about everything important
by the way the feet pedal urgently through his dreams,
I listen for awhile and then say,
"Another morning gone and the lawn not mowed,"

14. "About the Feet" from *In the Heart of Town, Still Digging*

and the feet leave the bed,
put on shoes
and sleepwalk through another day.

And the last poem I wrote for him refers to something he said a week or so before his death. He said he thought of himself as a weed, a dandelion, maybe, and he wondered what it was that a weed did. He thought about it for a few moments, and then he said that what a weed does is scatter seeds.

And that's what he did. He had a profound effect on the people who knew him closely. I have been amazed at all the folks who, after his death, told me things he had said to encourage or challenge or inspire them. But I was the one he shone on, and I am thankful for it, for having had the gift of love, the real thing, for all those years.

WHEN YOU WERE DEAD

Your last breath left me on a desert island
Leaves trembled in the whoosh, and dandelion fluff flew
 everywhere
The breeze pushed firmly on the boat, which slipped away
And so did you, into the fire
I have the island to myself now; the boat will not be back
I am like the tree in the forest, rooted and breathing
Where no one sees its leaves turn red and brown, then black
And no one hears its limbs come down, its heartwood crack
The shock of solitude has leveled me and kept me
Crawling the perimeter for miles around
Gathering pebbles in my skirt to build a house
Around the fire where I saw you disappear
You are only a vision now, seed fluff, blue smoke
And I am sore eyes beholding you, our body cleft
In the beginning was the word you spoke, no, all those words
And in the end, the word is all that's left
Food has been found at last in the interior

Pieces of cake, crumbs, butter in a drawer
But I need greens, iron, tonic, a springtime brew
And I am waiting for a gang of dandelions to muscle through.

People new to dream work are often frightened by dreams about dying, but what they usually indicate is that changes are coming about. Something needs to die in order for change to occur, for something else to come into existence. Death makes room for something new. And so we have a dream in which someone dies, or in which we ourselves die.

But no matter how much we desire change, we resist death, even the small death necessary to move life along. As the Spirit Toast Voice said, H_2O does not cry out when transformed from ice into steam, but people do.

At the time the local sexual assault survivor program was coming to an end, I had two dreams that bore on the situation. The first had a nightmarish quality that mirrored what was actually happening at the office:

NO REVIVING

I am being chased, hounded, accused of wrongdoing on the job.

Now there are a great many newly-dead bodies lying around. People are trying to set them back up, get them to keep working. Someone says it's hopeless to even try, because the animating spirit has gone from them and it's not possible to get it back.

Associations

WRONGDOING: I was a group facilitator and a board member, and I was trying to keep the program going. What we offered included long-term group work. This service was free. The hostile takeover was by the faction that favored short-term superficial support for the clients and referral to therapists for their deep work.

Therapists had only recently acquired the skills necessary to work with incest survivors, and they learned them from women like those in my office, who had learned from the pioneers in the field. But now the distress that survivors lived with had finally been codified and listed in the most recent diagnostic manual. Thus now only therapists were considered qualified to work with women who had suffered from childhood sexual abuse. Many women refused to work with a therapist, or to accept a diagnosis and an insurance company file that would remain in the system forever, and so these women were now on their own.

PROPPING UP THE DEAD: At the time of this dream I did feel as though I were propping up dead bodies and trying to breathe life into them. We had clients we had promised long-term support, and we were going to have to let them down. Because we knew so well what this would mean to them, it was a time of grief and stress for everyone.

The dream is telling me there is nothing I can do. I couldn't keep Vance from dying, and I couldn't keep the survivor program from dying. There are forces far beyond my ability to combat.

Nevertheless, several more months went by before my last client went on her way. Finally I had the following dream (see picture, next page):

LYING IN A CIRCLE

> We are all dead, my friends and I. Our bodies are lying on the ground arranged in a circle with our heads all pointing to the center.

Comments

The monoprint that I made to help my feelings along started out as a simple representation of the figures lying there dead in their shrouds, but in the press some inadvertent scratches on the plate turned the picture into one of a resurrection, which I then furthered with pencils.

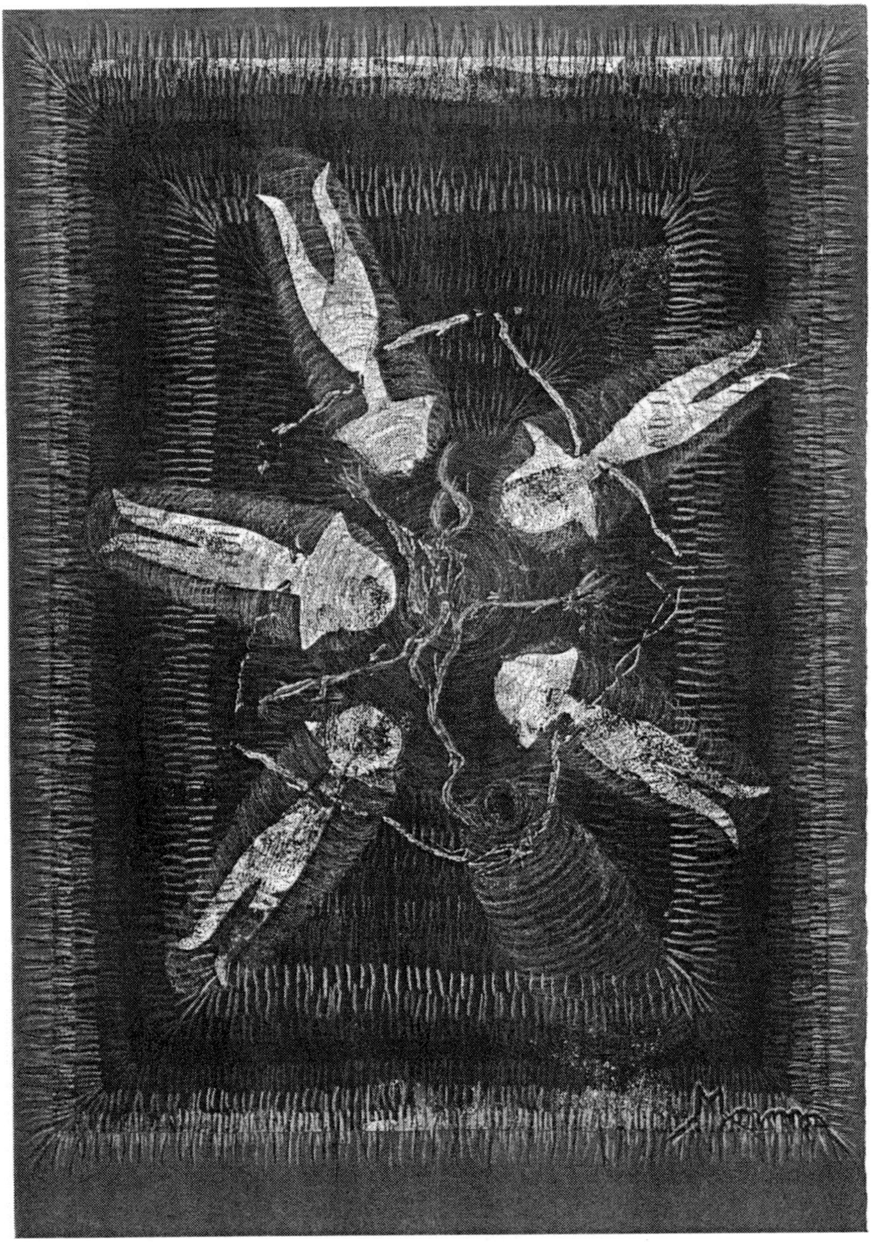

Lying in a Circle

The next dream lays out my deepest fear about death, which isn't really about death at all but about wasting my life:

CEASING TO EXIST

> I am sorting the experiences of my life into piles and wiping out some of the piles as easily as pressing a button, like deleting computer files. When they're gone, they're really gone, as though they never existed at all. When I erase a big batch, I feel blank for a moment, but that's all. Then I realize that none of them had any significance anyway. A horrible feeling washes over me.

Comments

The horrible sensation that ended this dream was like nothing I have ever experienced before: it is not describable. But to feel in my own body precisely what the desire for immortality is all about was quite an experience. *Thinking* that one's own existence matters no more than if one had never been born isn't so bad, but *feeling* it is the most profoundly negative sensation imaginable.

Another of the verses and ditties I memorized as a child was this one, and it states pretty clearly the task that life imposes. I don't know the title or author of this verse.

> Isn't it strange that princes and kings
> And clowns that caper in sawdust rings
> And common folk like you and me
> Are builders of Eternity?
> To each is given a bag of tools,
> A shapeless mass, and a book of rules,
> And each must make e're his life has flown
> A stumbling block or a stepping stone.

This is propaganda, of course, because no stepping-stone comes into being without its corresponding stumbling block, but the other possibility, that of making nothing but a blank of one's life, is surely the worst of all.

There is something of my frightening willingness to negate my own existence in the following dream:

FAILED SUICIDE

> I am a patient in a nursing home, and my future looks bad. I decide to commit suicide. This involves visiting my mother and getting one of the pills she's been hoarding for a time of need. I swallow the pill and wait for it to work.
>
> But as I wait, I think of all the pleasures of being alive, and I regret having to die. Whatever the reason was that I decided to take this pill, I've forgotten it now. I walk around looking at things I'll never see again, feeling pretty sorry for myself.
>
> But nothing happens. The pill doesn't work, and I don't die. Mother looks on in bewilderment. When I realize that the time has passed for me to be affected by the drug, I'm very happy and want to celebrate.
>
> I go back to the nursing home staff. The nurse won't celebrate with me, however. Instead she bawls me out for taking the pill in the first place. I look for the bearded doctor to tell him, but he is busy with other people.

Associations

NURSING HOME: Here's the nursing home again. Whatever is bad about my future is not clear, but I am pretty mobile, pretty able. I don't seem any more terminal than anyone else here, certainly not in bad enough shape to warrant suicide.

Maybe my problem is depression. Maybe my worst fear has come true and I'm like my fictional character, Mrs. Linton, unable to dance, with the emerald star hidden in her peed-on mattress, believing that the only way out is through the mortuary.

MOTHER: My mother allows me to escape whatever further obligations life will place on me by giving me one of her hoarded suicide pills. This could certainly be interpreted as a kindness, but again there's something not quite right about it. I'm much too spry in this dream to end it all. And I have learned to look twice at what Mother has to offer me in the way of escape.

But fortunately, the pill doesn't work. I'm not going to escape life that easily. The change that needs to happen here is not a death but a new lease on life, which is indicated by the fact that no one at the nursing home will celebrate with me. I need to *escape* from the nursing home, not *return* to it.

The nursing home was the locale for another of my stories, *Pastures White with Clover*,[15] in which the heroine did make it out the front door in her wheelchair, heading out to join her Own True Love, but she got lost and confused on the way and ended up wheeling around and around the block. The ending in this dream has a similar feeling to it. Something else had better happen.

And something does.

EUTHANASIA

> I have been brought to a place where a man is showing me around. He is extremely tall and thin and sallow. He wears a round, flat-topped, straight-sided cap with a tassel hanging down and dark clothing with a mandarin collar. Everything in the place is tall and thin: pole lamps and tables made of little circles of various heights. I walk

15. "Pastures White With Clover" was published in *The Minnesota Review*

around with this man as he tells me about the place.

The word for what this place is used for begins with the three letters "f u n" but I can't quite grasp the rest of the word. It seems important, and I try, but I just can't get it. It sounds like "funda" but I don't understand. We walk around as I look at things.

After awhile I begin to understand that I have been brought here to be euthanized. I try to figure out why. Who will benefit from my death? And now I remember that it was my male partner who brought me here.

Later: The scene has changed. On my deck at home most of the flowers have been killed by frost. The tuberous begonias under the ash tree, however, still have full, sturdy pink blooms. Nearby there are other flowers that seem to have turned to metal, very strong but delicate, like gold-leafing or like that jewelry made of leaves where the plant substance in the leaf veins has been extracted and replaced with gold or silver.

Associations

MALE PARTNER: It is my male partner, my inner man, who has brought me here, and this seems to be a beneficial act rather than an act of violence. The inner man is the person who, when he is doing what he should instead of making trouble, brings a woman to where she needs to go, to her center. He has a direct and personal interest in her. "You are my home," mine says. That indicates interest.

FLOWERS: This part of the dream came later, as though in answer to my question about benefit. The euthanasia is not to benefit the flowers that are dead or the ones still alive, but rather to transform the ones that are becoming gold and silver.

The euthanasia does not take place in this dream, however. I am suspicious. Is my partner planning to bump me off and collect the insurance? The question "Who benefits?" is not a bad question to ask. It can keep a person out of trouble. But whatever benefit is supposed to come is delayed by asking the question.

The question of benefit seems finally to be answered in the following dream:

DEATH AND DANCING

> A woman is dying. She's strong, and she fights hard to live. Her friends try everything they can do to keep her alive, but she finally dies anyway.
>
> Now I'm standing with my mother in line at the post office. There's an enormous expanse of marble floor. The man in line behind me strikes up a conversation with me and pretty soon we are dancing. He's short and strong, and he holds me tight so that my face is against the top of his head. I'm timid about this, but he's a very strong leader, so we whirl around and around that huge marble floor as though it were a ballroom. I feel a bit overwhelmed.

Comments

The death has come about, and I have left Mother behind while I dance on the marble floor of the post office with the man who whirls me around.

No longer am I hiding in the closet unable to dance. No longer am I asking the man to help me with Mother's love seat. Something else has happened.

The locale, the post office, reminds me of the mailboxes in my Central Ink hut. Standing in line means I'm mailing something. No longer am I hiding out, avoiding any presentation.

I wrote the following poem to describe the long period of desolation I endured before things got better:

DECOMPOSITION

How like an early winter
this new enterprise is turning out,
competencies dropping
like twigs from dry limbs.
A wind brings down
the last apples pecked hollow
by the black flock.
Branches follow.

Inside, the lamps are shrouded
in gray gauze. Sounds, too,
are wrapped in mask and muffler.
The smell is of dust.
Food is cold on the plate, and
underfoot, the sharpness
of small stones can be felt
at every step.

They say a state
like rapture comes out of this,
when dead wood sinks into itself
and every cell finds its rightful place,
scent to scent, touch to touch,
glance to glance, and when this
transformation is complete, we have
the light, the word, the bread, the wine, the dance.

PART 5

Coming Back Up

CHAPTER 17

The Dance

FLYING IN THE ORANGE DRESS

After dropping in unexpectedly on an old flame, I discover that I can fly by flapping the hem of the loose pale orange dress I'm wearing. It's delightful, and I spend most of the evening soaring gracefully around in my billowing dress, surprised that I can get off the ground so easily, and glad to be wearing a nice discreet white slip under the dress for modesty's sake.

I do stop flying long enough to say to one of the men who's present that he's a good man. He disagrees. "Well," I say, moderating my words, "you know how to be a good man, then." He nods.

When it's time to leave, I have someone else drive my car so that I can fly home.

Associations

DROPPING IN: To drop in unexpectedly on an old flame is an impulsive act indeed. What, no worrying about making his wife uncomfortable?

No fear that he might come on too strong? Following through on this impulse sets the stage for the rest of the dream.

FLYING: People tell me that flying is usually done in dreams by arm flapping, not skirt flapping. I wouldn't know. This is the first actual flying dream that I can remember.

Flying indicates the presence of Spirit. This is quite the opposite of the poor lyrebirds hung up in the clothing of my childhood. This pale orange dress is an improvement over the old dark blue, an orange not watered down or washed out but lightened by being mixed with white to make it look delicious, like a summer dessert. It fits, it's becoming, and I can fly in it.

CLOTHING: For many years I have been troubled, not surprisingly, by a crippling complex regarding my clothing. It is a manifestation of the Wallflower Woman complex, and it can make the simple act of getting dressed into an ordeal. It forbids me to beautify myself with clothing, and then it ridicules me for looking unattractive and upbraids me for trying to hide my unattractiveness in layers of dark clothing. Thus, faced with the moment of decision at the closet door, I can find nothing. I am frozen into immobility. But during the past few years I've had many occasions to confront this complex, and I do win a round of the struggle on occasion. Finding a garment I can fly in without being shot down is wonderful.

THE GOOD MAN: It's my inflated mood that's talking when I tell the man he's a good one, not an observation of his character. He corrects me, and rightfully so, but I continue to press for goodness. With my feet on the ground, I know quite well that a man is really a mixture of characteristics that can be either good or not so good, but in this dream I'm flying, and maybe they all look better than usual!

Another dream of clothing with the capacity to decrease the force of gravity is this one:

SHOES TO DANCE IN

I'm looking over the clothes in my closet, which seems to be the closet in my childhood room. I try on a denim patchwork vest that I like and decide to wear it with jeans and a turtleneck. I try on a pair of white shoes, and then I notice another pair on the closet floor. They're new, still wrapped in tissue paper, white and very delicate with satin ties and lace inserts. They look like dancing slippers or wedding slippers. When I put them on I discover that they have magical properties. I can leap and bounce high into the air. I'm delighted. I bounce across the hall to the room of a married couple to show them.

The room has changed since I saw it last: the clutter is gone and it is now tidy and attractive. The furniture includes the cherry wood bed from my first marriage.

Comments

What a change this dream is from my old NO MORE DANCING dream mentioned earlier, the one that occurred when I began recording dreams.

Bouncing into the room of a married couple has a significance that I did not catch at first. It is so easy to forget that each aspect of a dream is an aspect of oneself! But the "room of the married couple" within has been cleaned and tidied and furnished with the bed of the bride and groom. There is certainly no such room in the house of the Wallflower Woman.

Chalk up another victory at the closet door!

In the last dream of this section Vance and I are together again, with new living space being created for us:

HIGH RISE

Vance and I are at the premises of a new apartment that is being built for us. Workmen are here, one cutting some wood with a table saw. Vance picks me up and carries me. I feel very light in his arms, and when he tosses me into the air playfully, I rise quite high before he catches me.

Now I'm driving to a health club in the city. There's a steep hill on the way, and I accelerate to get up it. The car roars up and becomes airborne for a moment at the top before it levels off at an intersection.

I park the car and look for the health club. I've been here before, but there are two clubs, each located in a similar place, in buildings next door to each other. Since I'm not sure where to go, I check the lobbies of both buildings, then wait for the elevator in the one that feels right.

Associations

WORKMEN: Here are some of my inner masculine forces doing what they're supposed to do, building a high rise where I can live with my beloved. Their work is associated with another building that's going up, the New Church, which is both a dream image of mine and an actual building to house the congregation I belong to. In another recent dream I have fallen in love with one of the workmen; in still another the New Church has been completed and is officially ours.

Something new and valuable is going up within me. It has all the earmarks of a religious value.

CAR: This car not only makes it up the hill and becomes airborne but also levels off to be parked safely. While I have not been troubled by dreams in which my vehicle flies off into the stratosphere and can't get back to earth, some people are. Staying earthbound even when spirited is important. Otherwise the spiritual values are not connected to anything in one's actual life.

HEALTH CLUB: Here's my spa again, at long last, the place to rehabilitate and rejuvenate. When recovering after knee surgery, I went to a health club to exercise until my knee was strong enough to begin walking in the woods and hills and on the beaches again. I hated the health club, hated the machines, the sweat, the very idea of a "personal trainer." Going there felt like being in a revival meeting of somebody else's religion.

But in this dream I am choosing the health club that "feels right." This is an important difference. Such a club would help me make health-promoting choices, my personal trainer would understand my inner strengths and weaknesses and work with them in mind, and my whole person would benefit, not just my knee.

ELEVATOR: Finding the place that feels right and riding the elevator to the health club is an image that ought to lift a person out of the depression I was in when I began collecting these dreams. Indeed, it seems to have been happening.

CHAPTER 18

Destination

THE REAL THING

Traversing a large public market I am suddenly bumped by a bicycle. An oddly shaped child is walking it. She is only about a foot tall and has a very large head. The bicycle hits my anklebone and hurts. In a reflex act I swing my purse and hit the child. Now her grip on the bicycle wavers. I feel sorry about hitting someone so small, so I stop to help her get where she's going.

Now, at my childhood home I feel the impulse to look in one of the bookcases by the fireplace. "Why not?" I think, noticing both the impulse and my hesitation to act on it. I open the door, expecting to find the books that were there during my childhood.

But instead, the bookcase is filled with books in decorative bindings, mottled black and rose, a special edition. At first I think they are those blank books that people use for journals, but no, they have been printed. The flyleaves are made of handmade paper, and they're all published by the Writers' Center.

There's an informal group of people here. Several of the men are suitors. A new man joins the group. He too becomes a suitor. He's much larger than the rest of them, and he has a full voice and a commanding presence. The others do not stand a chance.

Now they are all out in the back yard. I am watching them through the dining room window over the desk. The tall man walks toward the house to come in. The moment is vivid. "This is *real*," I think. "This is the real thing. All the rest has been a dream."

Comments

This dream is different. The vivid ending that endures as I awaken is not something I'm used to; most of my dreams fizzle out into half-remembered scenes. Only BRINGING BACK BURIED JEWELS had that same sense of bringing something valuable from the dream world into waking life.

My thought, "This is real," connects with my long-standing quest for what is real and authentic. In the story *The Other Real World* the heroine brought a world into being that balanced the material (and materialistic) world of achievements and acquisitions, political power play and commercial development. My own authentic voice is an important goal of the quest.

Associations

PUBLIC MARKET: How interesting to have another dream that begins with encountering a child in the public market! But it's not surprising, because many dreams not included here have been pointing me toward the need to overcome my resistance to taking a public stand.

Individual public stands are what you find in such a market. My public stand displays my spiritual practice of imaginal work.

CHILD: Early in the formal part of the work I made the acquaintance of the child image that is part of myself. Mmmmm is the most vivid and vocal personification of it. But she is not the only manifestation. At the end of a yoga session one day, when I was lying on the floor, it felt as if a pressure in my chest had gathered into the form of a child who parted my ribs and pulled herself out like a creature emerging from a swamp. I made a clay figure to honor this image.

In dreams the child takes on different forms. Sometimes she is a new baby who can already talk. Here she is mostly head.

Why does she have such a big head? Could this be pointing to my own history in which the body had to be denied but the mind could be nurtured? Is this one of the givens of my life? Or maybe her importance is overstated: maybe she has a "swelled head."

Maybe this is a *wise* child, her large head like an owl's, and maybe this image presages the following dream and the picture on the next page:

THE FLIGHT OF OWLS

> The doc and I are invited to teach a seminar at a distant location. Transportation to the seminar will be no problem, because we are both owls and will fly there.

These are speculations, not assertions. Any image in a dream has many possible interpretations, and they can all be correct.

Jung speaks of the Child image as related to the lapis of the alchemists, the goal of the opus, the transpersonal Self. In the *Collected Works*, Jung writes of the Self, "The energy of the central point is manifested in the almost irresistible compulsion and urge to become what one is, just as every organism is driven to assume the form that is characteristic of its nature, no matter what the circumstances. This centre is not felt or thought of as the ego but, if one may so express it, the self." [16] The child is a representation of this Self that one is driven to become.

16. *Collected Works*, C. G. Jung, Volume 9, Part 1 Paragraph 634

The Big Head

BICYCLE: A bicycle requires above all balance. It seems natural that a representation of the inner core, the God-image, would choose such a vehicle. Gods by nature carry things to the extreme and need counterbalancing.

I am bumped by this creature with the bicycle. It isn't just that I seek the divine, but also that the deity seeks me. If people recognized that some of the bumps and blows that impede progress are actually nudges from the divine, it might be easier to respond in a helpful way. But here I do not recognize the rap on my ankle as anything divine at all, and I strike back with the full power of the purse.

Having done so, however, I see that this little person needs help, and I provide it.

The idea that God needs help is not something I learned as a child in Sunday School. But theology changes, and I have come to see God (or the gods) as Being-in-process, affected by what we do. I began to take more seriously the concept of the Holy Ghost, that breath of the Holy Spirit within each of us. Even the Old Testament states that humans were created in the image of God; with this creation story we can look at ourselves to see what God is like, and if we need help at times, so must God.

The implication here is that what one does contributes to God's continual creation and well-being, and this makes it understandable that the little core-person would bang my ankle to get my attention.

But what does God want? Specifically? From me?

In the dream I "help her get to where she's going," and that seems to be the right thing, given the rest of the dream.

Another dream sheds some light on my technique for helping someone to get where she is going:

LINED UP IN THE CROSS HAIRS

> My body is lined up in the cross hairs. It is a tight fit, but I feel centered here, with the cross of the cross hairs right at the level where the heavy stone is in place of my heart.

> Somehow, being here gives me a power I didn't have before: to direct people to the particular ferry they need, the one that takes them most expeditiously to where they're trying to go.

Comments

Although the fit is tight and being in the cross hairs sounds dangerous, by being centered myself I am able to help. Maybe this is something I am supposed to do, something my core self demands, like the woman in *The Other Real World* who is able to direct the daughter of the council member to the place where her own soul work could begin. Indeed, I have played a part in the work of others in many dream groups, imaginative writing classes, and other venues.

PURSE: Hitting this large-headed child with my purse implies spending money or other energy on her. This has most certainly happened. Mmmmm had many sessions with J and much of my time expended on giving her opportunities to express herself; this work has been fruitful indeed.

And what happens when I help the child? I find myself at my childhood home where important changes have come about.

BOOKS: The actual books in that bookcase in my childhood home were pretty paltry. We used the public library, not the bookstore. My father's library consisted of one book, a book that revealed his longing to get out of the factory: *Five Acres and Independence* by M. G. Kains.

It took writing to help me build a library of my own. The first story I wrote, the one about Mrs. Linton's birthday coming early, won first prize in the student literary contest, a lavish (to me) sum of money to spend in the bookstore. I came home with two shopping bags filled with books.

To have a special edition of books from the Writer's Center flanking the fireplace in my childhood home is clearly an improvement over the original situation.

JOURNALS: My actual journal volumes are printed-out sheets in three-ring notebooks, not handwritten cloth bound books, but they would more than fill the bookcases and they are certainly from this writer's center.

SUITOR: The Wallflower Woman did not have suitors (plural) to choose from; she had to take what she could get, like him or not. But here they are, the suitors, and one is clearly the best, the right one, the biggest, the one with the commanding voice. He has appeared in many dreams before, including this one:

THE MAN INSIDE

I'm alone in an apartment that has a large square sunken pool as its main feature, perhaps right in the living room. I float on my back in the pool, pushing off from one side, then the other, enjoying myself. The pool feels about ten feet square.

There's a window nearby covered with a Venetian blind. I get out of the water to adjust the blind, making sure it's closed completely. I also check the door to make sure it's locked. It's dark in the room.

Now, when I feel perfectly alone and safe, I am seized from behind. I can tell by the feel, the big hands, the strength and body size, that it's a man holding me, a very large man. He too is naked.

I'm scared, but instantly the fear rushes out of me and is replaced by super-awareness. I know that struggle and screaming will not help, so I relax to throw the man off guard while I make my plan.

Then we react to each other simultaneously: since I've relaxed, his hands become gentle, just as I reach for his genitals to hurt him. I feel the gentleness and warmth, and it tempers my attack so that I only squeeze his penis instead of doing real damage. It's stubby and small and very hard, and I pinch it, not for his pleasure but to make him let me go. He ejaculates. It continues for a long, long time.

Comments

Here he is, the real thing, a developing partnership with the one whose home I am, the inner one, the man behind me. The one whose importance to me grows and grows. (See picture, next page, *LOVE WITH THE SHADES DOWN.*)

Adjustments are necessary in order to encourage and sustain this partnership. In my dream, THE MAN BEHIND ME, where I was going down, down, down, when I realized that the man was in step behind me, I adjusted my movements to synchronize with his; in the dream above we synchronize our movements simultaneously.

The next dream indicated that this manuscript was coming close to its end:

DESTINATION

The locale is a large hotel somewhere on the coast. It's very old and well built, with wonderful old woodwork, including some inlaid structural support posts. It was the first building in the area, created as a destination resort. But now a town has grown up around it and the hotel is one of many.

My two daughters and my little grandson are here with me. We stroll around the town on streets that are sandy from the adjacent beach.

Inside the hotel I ask someone if the coastline is regular enough here to walk long distances along the shore.

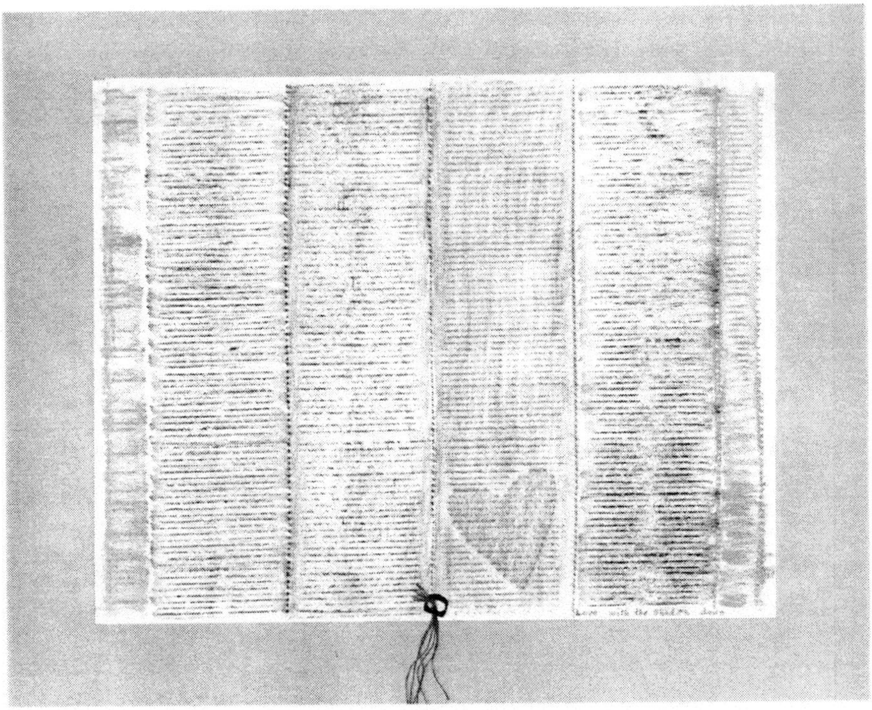

Love with the Shades Down

The answer is yes. I say that I live on the coast too, but you can't walk very far at a time on the beach because of the bluffs and headlands.

Now a saleswoman brings out a garment from the hotel dress shop. She wants me to buy it. I've already tried it on and although it is attractive, a one-piece pantsuit, I don't like the way it fits me. She adds a lavender colored scarf tied in a big bow to tempt me further, but I tell her that I've always been odd-sized and hard to fit and am even more so now that I'm bigger and older. She still doesn't quite give up, implying that I could lose a little weight and it would be perfect, but I shake my head no and she finally goes away.

Associations

THE COAST: The waters of unconsciousness meet the earth of everyday life at the shoreline. The place reminds me of the imaginative exercise I did when I went out onto the water but held to the shore during a windstorm. It also harks back to the poem "Where Mountains Rise out of the Sound."

THE DESTINATION: *Where I am going*, to this coastal place. The structural posts alleviate any anxiety about the strength of the structure, and their inlaid ornamentation makes it clear that the structure itself is part of the destination.

Whereas in the past many of my dreams were set in a house, more recently they take place in a more public setting, such as a hotel or convention center. In a recent dream scene, being part of something larger is represented this way:

ALL OUR CIRCLES MAKE THE LARGER CIRCLE

Our work is the construction of circles that are complete in themselves but can be opened to combine with other complete circles. Since the circles are abstractions, the

> only way to see what we have is by representations. The workman demonstrates the representation with small circles of blue thread that also can open to make a large circle.

When I wrote this dream down, I remembered the blue threads that had to be woven together just right in hedges.

THE TOWN: Here's the town again, this time a town grown up around this place *where I am going.*

MY FAMILY: The young ones are with me, even my grandson, who in a dream can be seen as an image of my young and growing inner masculine strength.

BLUFFS & HEADLANDS: These must be related to hedges. The inner bluffs I use to hamper my own progress. The head trips I use for the same purpose. That's why a coastline without them is still (and perhaps will always be) a destination.

DRESS: One's clothing, in a dream, can point to the Persona, that part of us that is an interface between the outer world and the inner self. The roles we play, the acts we put on to get along with others, our socialization.

Here someone is trying to sell me a garment, or role, that doesn't fit. Fortunately, I don't buy it. I accept myself as I am, odd shape and all, rather than try to fit into what this saleswoman thinks I ought to buy.

What might this mean for my Wallflower Complex that torments me at the closet door? I wrote the following poem as an exploration of that question:

WHAT I HEAR WHEN I LISTEN TO MY BODY

It is never easy, listening to the body.
Its voice is drowned out by commercials and advice
About what bodies are *supposed* to want:
Like food as medicine, or hunger for health's sake,

Pavement banging on unwilling feet,
The loss of precious moisture through the pores.

In some circles the talk is about tucks and plants and suction,
In others about *remedies* or *cleansing the system*,
About inhalations and ingestions and purifications.

The body itself has a different agenda.
This one says it does its own cleansing, thank you,
And it doesn't want to wake up from the knife
With parts missing.

Mornings I listen to what is said at the closet door.
"Soft fabrics," the skin tells me.
"No elastic," says the flesh. "Nothing tight."
The knees want warmth, the feet support;
The wrists say sleeves are never long enough.

These long arms always chilly at the wrist say
"You do not exist to hold the small."
Long legs won't mince, and toes recoil from
Decorator feet with silver nails.
Even at my age, the feet say "Stand firm, stand tall,
Stride along."

My growing hands say something of the same:
"You can handle more," they tell me.
"Buy big gloves,
And work, for the night is coming."

My torso has become the Venus of Willendorf, not de Milo,
Requiring more of everything, making outrageous demands:
"I would like to be tattooed with tulips," the spare tire urges
"Peonies," say the sagging breasts, "one red."

The ever-itchy spot on my shoulder blade has the last word.
"Just a wing pushing through," it says.
To my complaint about its flying me around in circles, it replies
"If you were meant to fly in a straight line, there'd be two."

The following dream provided me with a sense of what the next period of my life might entail:

THE NEW CHURCH

I am going through the stages of deeper and deeper membership in the New Church. I perform different tasks on the outer levels. Then, by means of a very casual promise, just a word or two signifying acceptance, I become married to the leader of the church, a formidable man I have seen only a time or two. This man seems as powerful and tall and distant as a foreign head of state, someone without a private life, someone who strides rather than walks. The marriage gives me access to the Inner Room.

On my way to the door of this room, which is concealed by a circuitous route, I suddenly remember that I'm already married to someone else. I'm distressed, thinking I will have to make this marriage known as soon as possible, and ashamed of getting myself compromised this way.

In the meantime, however, I continue past various large and busy groups of simple, pleasant people engaged in different church tasks until I reach the door to the Inner Room.

It's a large room. Someone is speaking from a podium. I can't hear what's being said. There are only a few chairs

> scattered informally around the room, as though a small attendance is what's expected, and all the chairs are taken except for the one chair that has been saved for me. I sit down.
>
> In the middle of the room is an empty chair, or rather a chair frame without a seat. I'm given to understand that this chair is left uncaned so that no one will try to fill it. It is purposely left vacant for the One Who Isn't Here, and this seems to be the central point of the religion.

Associations

NEW CHURCH: I have been working toward membership in the New Church for all these many years: imaginal work with a religious goal. And it's true that I have a clearer understanding of its discipline, its practices and rituals, its spiritual rewards.

One might ask where my Cold Fishy Eye is lurking. Could it have blinked shut?

No, it never blinks shut. But I finally learned how to circumvent it.

One Christmas, when my little grandson was still at the age to be afraid of "dat guy" in the red suit and certainly did not want him entering the house, via chimney or otherwise, his daddy consoled him, saying, "It's okay for you not to like Santa Claus. Santa likes you, and that's what counts."

I do not have to believe in any of this mumbo-jumbo. It's happening to me, and that's what counts. Again, what a relief! No longer must I browbeat myself into trying to believe things that are beyond my capacity for faith. When gifts were handed out, the gift of faith was given to someone else; I got the gift of doubt. But the process goes on, whether I believe in it or not. How clever of it!

THE PROMISE: The promise itself that resulted in the marriage is not spelled out in the dream, except that it signifies acceptance. Whatever it was, I must have believed that I could keep it. I don't make promises without that belief.

THE MAN: This man is not an ordinary man at all. He is larger than life and more important. I associate him with the best of the suitors, the man behind me, the one whose home I am, only this one is more of a figurehead rather than someone I would have a personal relationship with.

THE MARRIAGE: And the marriage is not ordinary either but rather a formality that assures me a place at the heart and core of the religion. In the Catholic religion, a woman who takes vows to be a nun becomes a bride of Christ. This is something like that.

That I am already married to someone else indicates that there is still plenty of work for me to do. I am divided in my commitment. And of course this is true.

MY CHAIR: I felt quite blessed to have a chair set aside especially for me. It reminds me of the red car that's especially for me in THE RED CAR AND THE CITY ON THE HILL. It also reminds me of the dreams I've had in which chairs have been denied me.

THE EMPTY CHAIR: But I found the empty chair to be the most interesting image in the dream, the place at the center saved for the One Who Isn't Here.

Will the One Who Isn't Here at the moment arrive later? Or is this a religion of seeking, or even yearning? Does the Holy One ever inhabit a temple or tabernacle permanently? I doubt it. Who hasn't known the absence of the Holy One?

THE HOLY ONE: This brought several comparisons to mind. One was certainly Moses' extensive preparation of the tabernacle, that portable pavilion in the desert, and the Lord God's taking up residence in it, finally, making His presence visible as a cloud by day and a fire by night.

Other comparisons that come to mind are in the ecstatic poetry of Kabir, with its longing for union with the divine, and TO PAINT THE PORTRAIT OF A BIRD, by Jacques Prévert, in which painstaking preparation must be made for painting the bird's portrait. If the preparations are sufficient, and through grace, the bird might sing.

The uncaned chair saved for the One Who Isn't Here is like the invitational space, the place you prepare with the greatest of care, because of your longing for the Guest, for the bird that sings, for Spirit, for union with the divine. My dream says that this is at the core of this New Church religion.

Important to this religion is to leave a place for what is missing. It sounds like my own church in outer life, Quimper Unitarian-Universalist Fellowship in Port Townsend, Washington. On a personal level, there is always a spot for the next person, a niche to fill, a place for the new person to place his or her best efforts. On an intellectual level, there is always a place for new truth and meaning, and on a spiritual level, we do indeed invite The Holy One.

I have been a UU since young adulthood, but was not very active in the local fellowship until after my husband died. One morning a woman from the congregation phoned me and suggested that I take a larger part, that they needed me. At that point, I needed them too, and so I began not only attending worship services regularly but also doing one thing and another to help out. This was a period of tremendous activity, as this small congregation built a church home with more than 8000 hours of volunteer, sweat-equity, labor.

I think the dream of THE NEW CHURCH and the building of this structure came together and opened up the new place for me to put my energy and commitment and love. The creation of a sacred space in the outer world went along with the inner work I've been doing. The Custodian has entered the church.

After the dream of THE NEW CHURCH, I thought this manuscript was finished. But Psyche had the last word with this dream:

DANCING IN THE TRASH

Once again I'm in a place of learning, a campus or workshop. I have the book people will be using in class, and

I'm looking for someone to give it to. I decide on a particular class member, and I write on a scrap of paper "This book belongs to ____" and start to write in her name. Then I think of someone else and start to write her name instead. Finally I realize that I can't tell who needs this book the most, so I decide to put it out for anyone who wants it.

There's a lot of stuff on the floor, a real mess. I mutter "garbage, garbage, garbage." I consider tidying it up, but don't do it. Instead I prance through it like a kid jumping in piles of raked-up leaves, dancing around and singing "Dancing through the trash, dancing through the trash, we will come rejoicing, dancing through the trash" at the top of my voice to the tune of "Bringing In The Sheaves." (See picture, next page.)

Dancing in the Trash

Afterword

It would be utterly false of me to pretend that my difficulties have ended. I am convinced that indeed there is no happy ending that does not precede another difficult beginning. Many times after writing this book I found myself sitting on the same old block, feeling dried out and lifeless, worthless, as though the juice had been sucked out of me.

But again and again I came to recognize the symptoms. Again and again I would read old journals and find descriptions of how I had worked through it all before. And again I would notice that my mother had been appearing in my dreams, innocuously, of course. And finally I would get it.

When this happens, I have to start again. I have to make the effort to follow whatever impulses come along without becoming distracted, without waiting, without doing something else first. Each effort I make in this direction strengthens me until at last I regain my competence and get back to work. What used to take months now takes a few days.

None of this could happen if I did not do my dream work as a regular spiritual practice. I begin every day writing in my journal, whatever dream I can remember first, then whatever I can add to the dream, and finally an account of yesterday's events. This practice enriches my life.

Bibliography for Inner Work

Where People Fly and Water Runs Uphill, by The Rev. Jeremy Taylor, a Unitarian Universalist minister. About using dream work to tap the wisdom of the unconscious. Some chapter titles are:

What You Should Know About Dreams: Ten Basic Assumptions
Exploring the Many Layers of Dreams: The Basic Assumptions in Action
Techniques for Improving Dream Recall
Working with Dreams in Groups

Dream Work, also by The Rev. Jeremy Taylor. This author brings together a number of ways to work with dreams from different sources. His passion for the work is evident in his writing.

Inner Work, by Robert A. Johnson, Jungian analyst and author of several books in the field. *Inner Work* is about using dreams and active imagination for personal growth. Contains helpful introductory material as well as instructions for working with dreams and active imagination. "Active imagination" is the dialogue one can enter with the different parts of oneself that appear as other characters in dreams.

At A Journal Workshop, by Ira Progoff, Jungian scholar, writer and developer of the Intensive Journal program at Dialogue House. Use the

Revised Edition that teaches process meditation. Sections of the book include Preparing, First Stages, Life/Time Dimension, Dialogue Dimension, Depth Dimension, Meaning Dimension, Continuing, and Appendices.

The Penguin Dictionary of Symbols, by Jean Chevalier and Alain Gheerbrant, translated by John Buchanan-Brown. An 1150-page paperback crammed with information about the many symbolic meanings attributed to every kind of thing. A bargain at $20.

The Herded Symbol Dictionary, translated by Boris Matthews. A pocket-sized paperback published by Chiron Publications with more than 1,000 entries and 450 illustrations.

A Dictionary of Symbols, by J. E. Cirlot, translated from Spanish by Jack Sage. A scholarly discussion of the symbolic meanings of everything from "abandonment" to "zodiac."

The American Heritage Dictionary, third edition. This is the dictionary that carries the etymology of the English language back to the Indo-European roots of those words that are descended from these roots. A wonderful source of related words.

Anatomy of the Psyche: Alchemical Symbolism in Psychotherapy, by Edward F. Edinger, Jungian analyst, psychiatrist, teacher and writer. Not an easy book but fascinating and filled with information. Edinger writes clearly about the process by which one's psyche develops.

Tracks in the Wilderness of Dreaming, by Robert Bosnak, a Jungian analyst specializing in dream work. This one compares Bosnak's method of dream work with that of an Aboriginal spirit doctor and gives practical suggestions for working with your own dreams.